STARTING & RUNNING
A SUCCESSFUL
CONSULTANCY

If you want to know how ...

Going for Self-employment
How to set up and run your own business

The essential guide for anybody who wants to set up a business. It spells out the pros and cons of self-employment; assesses the risk involved; and offers solutions to raising finance, managing resources and complying with regulations.

Starting Your Own Business
The bestselling guide to planning and building a successful enterprise

'Encouraging and practical, Green's book covers all the basics ... An entrepreneur himself Green knows the questions to ask. He includes useful guidelines about remaining positive in the face of setbacks.' – Management Today

Work for Yourself and Reap the Rewards
How to master your destiny and be your own boss

'The book is written in a clear, concise and readable format. It's also very enjoyable.' – CEO, Business Enterprise Agency of South East Essex Ltd

Please send for a free copy of the latest catalogue:

How To Books
Spring Hill House, Spring Hill Road
Begbroke, Oxford OX5 1RX, United Kingdom
info@howtobooks.co.uk
www.howtobooks.co.uk

SUSAN NASH

STARTING & RUNNING
A SUCCESSFUL
CONSULTANCY

How to build and market your own consulting business

REVISED AND UPDATED · 3RD · THIRD EDITION

'I developed the methodology in this book to build my own extremely successful consultancy business; and I've taught many others how to do it too.'

how to books

With thanks to Courtney Bolin for her interactive layout of the book.

Published by How To Books Ltd,
Spring Hill House, Spring Hill Road,
Begbroke, Oxford OX5 1RX.
Tel: (01865) 375794. Fax: (01865) 379162.
info@howtobooks.co.uk
www.howtobooks.co.uk

First edition 2003
Second edition 2005
Third edition 2007

British Library Cataloguing in Publication Data
A catalogue record for this book is available from the British Library

ISBN 978 1 84528 216 5

Cover design by Baseline Arts Ltd, Oxford
Produced for How To Books by Deer Park Productions, Tavistock
Typeset by PDQ Typesetting, Newcastle-under-Lyme, Staffs.
Printed and bound by Cromwell Press Ltd, Trowbridge, Wiltshire

NOTE: The material contained in this book is set out in good faith for general guidance and no liability can be accepted for loss or expense incurred as a result of relying in particular circumstances on statements made in the book. The laws and regulations are complex and liable to change, and readers should check the current position with the relevant authorities before making personal arrangements.

Contents

Preface

How to use this book

> If one advances confidently in the direction of his dreams, and endeavours to live the life which he has imagined, he will meet with success unexpected in common hours.
>
> *Henry David Thoreau*

Why consulting?

The business environment is changing drastically. No longer is there long-term employment and job security. Consulting has become a viable and growing working option for individuals since the 1990s. However consulting does not provide a miracle solution to work options. *The Successful Consultant* is designed as a workbook containing a wide variety of exercises that you can complete to help you make a consulting career for yourself a reality not just a possibility.

Who can this book help?

This book has been written for professionals, with specific functional knowledge, experience or expertise, who wish to evaluate whether they want to be consultants and consider an alternative lifestyle to full-time work. So this book is for:

- Individuals who are debating leaving 'corporate life' and want to explore alternative career options.
- Consultants who are running their own business who want to increase their market share and revenue.
- People between jobs who wish to generate income.
- Entrepreneurs in the making who wish to begin an independent lifestyle.
- Those who are looking for greater flexibility and more choices in the work they wish to do.

What will you achieve by using this book?

After reading this book, you will:

◆ Have a clear understanding of consulting and the entire consulting process.
◆ Understand the benefits and challenges of consulting as a career choice.
◆ Learn how your own strengths and challenges fit with the consulting lifestyle.
◆ Be able to define and establish the strategic direction for your consulting business.
◆ Be able to create and implement a marketing strategy.
◆ Learn skills and practical tools to find clients and close deals.
◆ Understand how to raise finances and maintain financial control of your business.
◆ Be able to balance on-going business while maintaining the marketing process to avoid the 'feast or famine' syndrome.
◆ Know how to organize your consulting business.
◆ Have paying clients!

Exercise P.1   What do you want to achieve using this book? To help you identify what you want to achieve from using this book, answer the following questions:

◆ What are you doing currently? Are you just starting out? Have you been a consultant for a while?
◆ What would you like to learn from reading this book?
◆ What would you like to do as a result of using this book?
◆ What would you like to achieve?
◆ Which of the objectives above most appealed to you and why?

Coaching point
Defining your goals for reading this book will help focus your attention in the areas that are of the most interest to you.

So now you have decided what you want to achieve, let's look at how you can use this book to make it happen.

Through the rest of the book we will introduce the principal concepts, knowledge and information you require interspersed with exercises, within specific areas, to become a successful consultant. Then we will use checklists and discussion questions to help you implement the key ideas. In addition, we will follow four people as they evaluate whether they wish to be consultants, and as they make a start in the consulting profession. Extra examples will be provided where necessary to clarify points.

The book is hands on, and throughout you will find the material organized into several categories designed to create a learning experience that is interactive, inspiring, informative, and clear.

The information types include:

Game plan
An overview of what you will achieve within each chapter.

Exercises
Activities that can be used to try out material and put concepts to work.

Foul!
To clear up a perception that may not be accurate.

Coaching point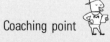
A note or reminder about what to do or look for as you try out the material.

Time out!
A clarification or side note.

Scorecard

A series of questions to help you review outcomes from each chapter.

What's in this book?

This book comprises four main sections.

◆ **Section one: getting started**. This section includes setting the scene on the consulting industry, evaluating your fit, deciding what type of consulting business you want to run and what you want success to look like. While the content could appear too high-level, time invested in this section will help secure a clear business direction.

◆ **Section two: getting clients**. This section includes the part that most prospective consultants either miss or avoid: getting clients! This section includes practical tips to reduce the fear of selling and open up market opportunities in the most time-efficient way.

◆ **Section three: getting money**. This section covers the content which most people gravitate towards – how much to charge and how to collect fees. Most of us want to make money as a consultant – this section will help you do that!

◆ **Section four: getting organized**. This section describes techniques for organizing your business including getting your office set up, structuring consulting assignments and creating your consulting action plan. Unlike a 'real job' there is no company structure – you have to do all the organizing yourself!

Where to start

The following approach is recommended to optimize your use of this book.

1. Read Chapter 1: Setting the Scene. This chapter and its exercises will help to clarify what we mean by consulting. If you are an existing consultant, you can then choose which section of the book you think would help you most in your current business situation. If you are a new consultant, we recommend completing Section One in its entirety before moving on to other sections.

2. Use the section most relevant to you. From this point the choice is yours, choose the section in which you have the most interest and jump in!

3. Complete the exercises. Many of the concepts described in this book are self-evident, but just because they are common sense does not mean that they are common practice. Spending time completing the exercises can help to surface issues and enable you to make behaviour changes.

4. Share the exercises with those who are close to you. As we discuss later in this book, having a support structure is a critical differentiator between making the grade and failing as a consultant. Working through these exercises with those who are part of your support structure can not only help you to surface other issues, but can increase the mutual understanding of what you are doing and why!

> If you can imagine it, you can achieve it. If you can dream it, you can become it.
>
> *William Arthur Ward*

What else?

Feel free to make the book your own: write in the spaces provided, complete the exercises and make a note of your learning. Remember, any behaviour change needs constant reinforcement: use this book as one of the tools in your toolkit in achieving consulting excellence!

As a result of reading this book you will be able to evaluate whether consulting is an option you wish to consider. If you decide yes, then this book will give you an understanding of the steps you need to take to create a successful consulting business. I made the decision in 1994 and would never go back. Good luck!

Susan Nash

'Susan's book was extremely informative. I came away with simple, valuable tips that have produced fantastic results for my small business.'

From Rufus F Branson, The Branson Group LLC

'Susan has a wealth of experience which is presented in an interesting interactive format.'

Patti McDonald

'Susan's no-nonsense approach helped me get on the right foot as I was starting my business practice. Even though it has been over six years, I continue to refer to Susan's ideas. Her book presents you with a framework to set up and manage your consulting business. And what's even better, you don't have to go through pages and pages of generally known information to get to the good stuff. It is all good.'

Julia Bushkov, HR Ventures

SECTION ONE:
Getting Started

CHAPTER ONE

Setting the Scene

 Game plan

The purpose of this chapter is to:

◆ Explain why the current business environment is conducive to becoming a consultant.

◆ Describe the self-employed market.

◆ Define, for the purpose of this book, what we mean by consulting.

◆ Understand the advantages and disadvantages of working for a consulting firm.

◆ Introduce the case studies that we will be following throughout the book.

The business environment in the new millennium

Business life is changing drastically and these changes are creating new opportunities in the world of work, which is moving from a stable business environment in earlier decades to radical, complex and increasing change. Thirty years ago companies saw the future as somewhat predictable and manageable with gradual incremental change. Change occurred in a linear fashion where one cause produced only one effect, with a simple additive property, i.e. $1 + 1 = 2$. Change now is being driven from a variety of perspectives and is happening exponentially. There are non-linear relationships between causes and effects, where there can be multiple solutions to one problem and there is synergy with the interaction of the parts, i.e. $1 + 1 = 4!$

Time out!

Did you know that...

◆ On average, individuals now have eight careers in their working lives.

◆ The economic base has changed from industry to information – in the US to make a computer chip requires 98% skills, ideas and knowledge and 2% energy and raw materials.

◆ In 1984 the average product development cycle lasted three years. In 1990 it dropped to 18 months. In 1997 it was six months and still falling.

◆ High school graduates have been exposed to more information than their grandparents were in a lifetime.

◆ Every two or three years the knowledge base doubles.

◆ It used to take 7–14 years for half of a worker's skills to be outdated. Today, it only takes three years for 50% of our skills to be outdated.

Some of the causes of change are:

◆ global competition
◆ technological advances
◆ decreasing product life cycles
◆ multiple communication channels
◆ expectation of instant/24 hour availability
◆ change from manual to cerebral skills (70% of all jobs in Europe and 80% of all jobs in the USA will require cerebral skills)
◆ virtual elimination of 'jobs for life'.

The Shamrock Organization

As these changes are taking place the 1980s and 1990s saw a drastic restructuring in the economic workplace. David Birch describes this phenomenon as 'atomizing', where more and smaller businesses are performing the work that fewer and larger organizations did before. This strategy provides organizations with greater flexibility, reduction in costs (ensuring full-time people are not employed in quiet times) and greater adaptability. This atomizing has brought many changes to the way people work. At least 1 in 10 people were

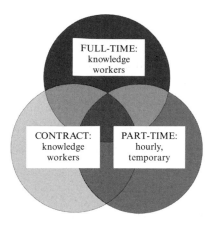

Fig. 1.1 Shamrock Organization.

self-employed in the UK in 2002 according to a Labour Market Trends report in 2003.
Charles Handy, in his book *The Age of Unreason*, talked about the Shamrock
Organization of the future (see Figure 1.1) which comprises three key components:

♦ Full-time knowledge workers with specialized expertise.
♦ Part-time, hourly or temporary workers who are flexible and provide less complex
  skills.
♦ Contract workers who also possess specialized expertise but who provide this on a
  consulting or contract basis.

The new self-employed market

No bird soars too high if he soars with his own wings.

William Blake

With the recession of the 90s, and collapse of the perceived employment contract between
employers and employees, there has been an enormous jump in the number of people
classified as self-employed.

Time out!

Did you know that:

◆ In the UK the self-employed workforce comprises approximately 3.4 million people, 12.5% of the workforce contributing an estimated 55 billion pounds to the country's economy according to the Inter-Departmental Department Register in 2002.

◆ The businesses which do best in the self-employed market are service businesses which historically require lower start-up costs and less capital overhead, according to Godfrey Golzen in the *Daily Telegraph, Working for Yourself Book*.

The role of consulting is part of the self-employed service industry. Consulting remains a lucrative growth industry for those who are able to innovate for their clients' benefit and it continues to be a productive outlet for thousands of solo practitioners who choose this profession over a 9-to-5 job working for someone else.

Defining consulting

Building up small businesses is the toughest job in the world.

Tim Waterstone, Founder of the Waterstone's bookshop chain

Before we begin discussing consulting in more depth, spend a few moments to answer the questions below and then compare your answers with the later sections in this chapter and the next.

Exercise 1.1 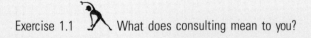 What does consulting mean to you?

What do you understand by the term consulting?

_____

_____

What is attracting you to the possibility of consulting at this time?

_____

_____

What do you perceive to be the benefits of consulting over a full-time position?

_____

_____

Coaching point

Individuals are attracted to consulting for different reasons. Understanding why you are considering consulting, and the benefits you expect, can enable you to assess objectively whether the reality of consulting is going to match your ideal.

Consulting is a service business, which means that:

◆ The deliverable is somewhat intangible (there may be tangible components such as products).
◆ It is harder to standardize.
◆ The person providing the service plays a considerable role in the success of the service.
◆ It requires less start-up costs and often lower overheads – it can be you and an office!

Time out!
Consulting can be defined as _providing independent services to meet a variety of clients' needs in exchange for money._ The critical factor is _money._

Foul!
There will always be lots of opportunities for helping clients, but ensuring these clients are willing to pay is critical. While some individuals believe that giving away services is a way to establish a client base and get started, you are devaluing your services by not charging for them. Free consulting generates lots of demand for…more free consulting!!

Deciding to charge a lower rate to clients in the beginning stage of your business is a strategy we will discuss and evaluate in Chapter 7.

The types of services that consultants provide will vary from industry to industry and individual to individual, and will include such support as problem-solving, assessing needs, making recommendations, providing additional resources and implementing ideas. Consulting can be viewed as a state of mind: a common approach to a situation whether you are internal or external to an organization. Consultants can range from, to name but a few:

◆ Strategic planning consultants who help organizations define their vision and direction.

◆ Process reengineering consultants who provide support evaluating and recommending process improvements.

◆ Training consultants who provide services such as training programmes and curriculum development.

◆ Computer consultants who may assess current systems effectiveness, and recommend or implement systems improvements.

◆ Marketing consultants who help design new product improvements and design product launch strategies.

Time out!
Consulting is defined as different from contracting because, among other things, consultants:
◆ have more than one client
◆ are not told how, just what
◆ have their own place of work
◆ are responsible for their own output.

Consulting is growing as organizations focus on their areas of speciality and use consultants to provide additional services. Many consulting companies originate when organizations lay off individuals and then use their services on a contract basis. Oracle has its own consulting division, and yet many consulting companies have sprung up to supplement its services.

Because of the many changes in the business industry, there are many more consultants today than ever before.

Time out!

The *consulting industry* is diverse, unregulated and broken into several categories:

◆ Large national and multinational firms employing more than 50 consultants, e.g. strategic consulting firms such as McKinsey and Company, and Bain and Company, and offshoots from large accounting firms such as KPMG, Bearing Point, etc.

◆ Medium-sized firms employing between ten and 50 consultants.

◆ Individual practitioners. *Venture* magazine (a US publication for small business start-ups) estimates that more than half of all consulting firms are one-person operations.

◆ Internal consultants. These consultants work with only one company's divisions, subsidiaries and new acquisitions. The money they receive is their salary.

◆ Public Agency consultants such as the General Accounting Office and the Service Core of Retired Executives provide consulting both to private and public businesses and to Government agencies.

◆ Individuals between jobs.

In fact, the following statement is often heard, 'If you can't do the work, you teach. If you can't teach, you consult!'

Working for a consulting firm

To find out what one is fitted to do, and to secure an opportunity to do it is the key to happiness.
John Dewey

If you are not familiar with the consulting industry, working for a consulting firm can be a good way to get started. Below are listed the advantages and disadvantages of working for a consulting firm.

Advantages	Disadvantages
◆ Clients are given to you.	◆ Many of the perceived disadvantages of ordinary full-time work are present.
◆ Billing and collection of payment is done for you.	
◆ There is regular, dependable money.	◆ There will be the same amount of politics as any other organization.
◆ This can provide an opportunity to learn the business.	◆ It is just another job.
◆ Other resources are available such as copying, stationery, office space and equipment, etc.	◆ The pay will not be as high.
	◆ You will have no opportunity to select clients.
◆ You do not have to worry about taxes, as most consulting firms will pay you and deduct taxes at source.	
◆ Marketing is done for you.	

For the purposes of this book, we will be looking at the consulting market comprised of one-person consulting firms.

Exercise 1.2   Would you benefit from working for a consulting firm?

Answer the following questions to give you some insight as to whether working for a consulting firm would be a useful strategy to consider as you begin your consulting career.

Yes   No

☐ ☐   Have you ever worked for a consulting company?

☐ ☐   Have you ever worked for a small business?

☐ ☐   Have you had direct contact with paying customers?

☐ ☐   Have you had budgetary responsibility for costs and expenses?

☐ ☐   Have you been involved in generating revenue from customers?

☐ ☐   Have you worked in a department where you had little logistical support?

☐ ☐   Have you had to do your own invoicing and collection at any time?

☐ ☐   Have you had to work with no structure?

☐ ☐   Have you ever worked in an environment where you decided your own workload?

◆ If you answered no to more than six questions, you may want to carefully assess whether you would benefit from working with a consulting company to 'learn the ropes'.

◆ If you answered yes to more than six questions, this could indicate that you have experienced a similar environment to the one in which you may be consulting and therefore you would not necessarily benefit from working for a consulting company.

◆ Based on this assessment, make a note below of what appeals to you in working for a consulting firm.

_____

_____

◆ What concerns you about working for a consulting firm?

_____

_____

◆ What will you do as you get started?

_____

_____

Coaching point

Even if you answered no to many of the questions, this is no reason not to try independent consulting: you may be at the right point in your life to face the challenge. In the same way, you may choose to work for a consulting firm even if you answered 'yes' more frequently as a different way to get started and build a network of contacts and some credibility with successful client engagements. There is no definitive correct or incorrect approach!

Case studies

As we previewed in the introductory section, we will be following the paths of four individuals as they begin their consulting careers. The purpose of these case studies is to bring to life some of the challenges that individuals faced, and to make real the ideas and concepts introduced in each chapter.

Joe

Joe has worked in high-tech marketing helping organizations launch products in a timely manner. He enjoys the challenge of product marketing, but feels that the environment of working in an organization, moves far too slowly for him. He is thinking of consulting to see if he can get more reward for what he does and create more time off for himself.

Frank

Frank is a hardware engineer who has been working for a high-tech company for several years. As the technical support business began to be more challenging, with shorter product life cycles and more push to generate revenue as well as ensuring customer satisfaction, he decided to begin to evaluate different working options. He has begun to run classes for the local college on how to reengineer support centres. He now has what appears to be a demand for his services on a contract basis and he wants to decide whether to start his own consulting business or to pass on the work to other colleagues who are currently independent.

Julia

Julia has spent over 20 years in the human resources field, covering all the basic HR functions: benefits, compensation, employee relations and legal compliance. She has worked in both large and small companies and therefore understands the complexities and needs inherent in both types of corporate environment. Most recently, she has worked for a start-up that has gone public and she now has a reserve of shares which means that she does not have to work full time for a while. She is considering consulting as a more flexible working alternative.

Marie

Marie is 39 and has been in the training business for over 15 years. She spent seven years with a training company, which grew from three people to 100, during which time she was in the sales and marketing section. When she left the training company she worked for another company on the implementation side running training programmes and designing curricula. She then joined a retail company as Director of Training but is wondering whether running her own training consulting firm would be a more lucrative and rewarding option.

Checklist

1. Did you define consulting and identify why you are interested in it?
2. Did you consider working for a full-time consulting firm?

Scorecard

Before moving on to Chapter 2, think about the following questions:

◆ When you defined consulting, what attracted you to consulting at this point and how objective were you in that assessment? To what extent were you imagining an unrealistic upside to consulting as a career? How could you be more realistic in your assessment of consulting as an option?

◆ When you evaluated working for a consulting firm, what insights did you gain from that exercise? What could working for a consulting firm provide to you as a career choice? What were the disadvantages you were most aware of? How can you get the best of both worlds: independent consulting and working for a company?

Evaluating Your Fit

 Game plan

The purpose of this chapter is to:

◆ Identify the strengths and possible challenges inherent in pursuing an independent consulting career.

◆ Present the characteristics of successful consultants.

◆ Enable you to assess your strengths and possible challenges as a consultant.

◆ Decide a plan of attack for the rest of this book.

Being realistic about consulting

> Hard work spotlights the character of people: some turn up their sleeves, some turn up their noses, and some don't turn up at all.
>
> *Sam Ewig*

Often when professionals consider consulting as a profession, they see only the money that other consultants charge and focus on the advantages of consulting as an alternative to corporate employment. In reality, running your own consulting business has certain advantages and disadvantages. It is important to understand and consider both to ensure you capitalize on the advantages and manage the disadvantages. Being honest with yourself and keeping your eyes open will increase your chances of building a successful consulting business.

Exercise 2.1 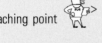 Consulting advantages and disadvantages

Let's see how you perceived the advantages of consulting as a possible career choice. Go back to Exercise 1.2, the second and third questions.

What do you perceive to be the benefits of working as an independent consultant?

_____

_____

What do you perceive to be the possible disadvantages of working as an independent consultant? You may want to involve significant others in your life in this discussion!

_____

_____

Coaching point

It can be very tempting to view consulting as the solution to all evils, the 'miracle cure' -- particularly if you have just experienced a difficult redundancy situation. However, in reality there are many disadvantages to a career as a full-time consultant. Being aware of these can help you avoid them.

Advantages and disadvantages of consulting

On page 16 are listed some of the advantages and disadvantages that need to be evaluated when considering consulting as a full-time career.

Foul!

One of the most common false assumptions is that you will earn more money and have greater flexibility in hours – time off when you feel like it. Unfortunately that doesn't factor the client into the equation who *always* has a critical project they want you to work on as soon as you try to take a holiday or day off!

Advantages of consulting	Disadvantages of consulting
◆ flexibility in hours and clothes	◆ uncertain and variable income – feast or famine
◆ creativity in projects	◆ hard to find clients
◆ diversity in work	◆ always looking for work – constant marketing
◆ higher pay (when working)	
◆ able to work own hours to match body clock	◆ must perform all tasks: marketing, finance, etc
◆ focus on work you like to do	◆ no work, no pay
◆ no performance reviews	◆ taxes can be a problem – time consuming and detail oriented
◆ can choose work associates and environment	
◆ fewer politics	◆ hard to get accurate feedback
◆ see the result of the work you do	◆ very vulnerable to business cycles
◆ get paid for the work you do not your political savvy	◆ many bosses
	◆ must be self-motivated
◆ higher challenges	◆ no holiday pay
◆ less constrained by a job description	◆ must be healthy
◆ greater impact	◆ must handle rejection
◆ can hide money for retirement	◆ lonely/isolated
◆ in control of your own destiny	◆ you have to self-train and pay for any training you do
◆ project orientation with a beginning, a middle and an end	
	◆ it can be like starting a new job every day
◆ wider opportunities	
◆ there is an opportunity for continuous learning	◆ may be difficult getting clients to pay on time
◆ more time off.	◆ pay your own benefits
	◆ no support services
	◆ it's hard to leave work behind
	◆ the need to constantly shift between projects and other tasks.

Exercise 2.2 Consulting advantages and disadvantages to you

◆ Take a moment and review the previous list. Pick out the advantages that most appeal to you and list them below. Are these realistic in your current situation?

◆ Now think about the disadvantages with which you most identified. How could you minimize these disadvantages so that they don't trip you up?

<table>
<tr><th>Advantages</th><th>Disadvantages</th></tr>
<tr><td>_____</td><td>_____</td></tr>
<tr><td>_____</td><td>_____</td></tr>
<tr><td>_____</td><td>_____</td></tr>
<tr><td>_____</td><td>_____</td></tr>
</table>

Case study: Marie

Marie has evaluated the strengths and weaknesses of consulting for her and believes that the benefits of reduced politics, greater challenge, control of the end product and variety of projects will overcome the potential disadvantages of needing a consistent revenue stream due to both children being at college.

Coaching point

Make sure you include those who are important to you in these discussions. You may perceive lots of travel to be a benefit; those who are left at home to 'man the fort' may not necessarily agree with you!

Not only does a consulting career involve certain advantages and disadvantages but there are certain key characteristics that contribute to successful consultants.

Characteristics of successful consultants

The entrepreneur is essentially a visualizer and an actualizer. He can visualize something, and when he visualizes it he sees exactly how to make it happen.   *Robert L. Schwartz*

Consulting is a demanding profession and the requirements for success are therefore also demanding.

Time out!

A study by the Association of Management Consultants entitled *Personal Qualifications of Management Consultants* found the following attributes essential for successful consultants:

- understanding of people
- integrity
- courage
- objectivity
- ambition
- problem-solving ability
- judgment
- ability to communicate
- psychological maturity
- good physical and mental health
- professional etiquette and courtesy
- stability of behaviour and action
- self-confidence
- intellectual competence
- creative imagination.

Robert E. Kelley, in his book *Consulting*, has summarized eight categories for successful consultants.

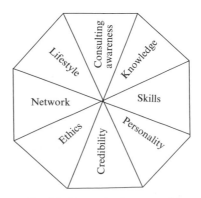

Fig. 2.1. Categories for successful consultants.

To accomplish great things, we must not only act, but also dream: not only plan, but also believe.

Anatole France

1. Consulting process awareness

Simplistically, as a consultant, you need to be able to:

- market your service
- deliver your service
- organize your administration
- be an accountant.

However, in reality it is important to understand that consulting is a process with a series of stages. Each stage has a series of tasks that must be performed. At any one time, you need to be marketing, meeting with prospects, writing proposals, 'doing the real work', billing, collecting revenue, keeping your office organized and ensuring your services are smoothly delivered.

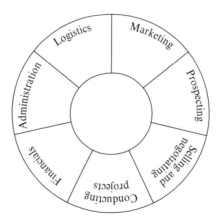

Fig. 2.2 Consulting process activities.

Foul!

The number one reason that consultants experience feast or famine is because they forget to continue marketing when they are working on one or multiple client projects. No matter how busy you are with clients, all the other activities need to take place!

When you work for an organization, you often only have to work in a couple of areas. Your understanding of, and your ability to work simultaneously in, all steps of the process are critical to your overall business success. Most consultants fail because they fail to 'multiplex' adequately, and then neglect critical aspects of their business.

Case study: Marie

Marie has worked for a training-consulting firm as it grew from three people to over 100 employees. She has spent some time being an independent consultant, has worked as Director of Training for a retail company, and is now considering starting up her own consulting business again. During her employment she has continued providing limited consulting services for other clients, negotiating time off without pay from her employer. Because of her work with the training company, she has an excellent knowledge of the consulting process and possesses excellent sales and marketing skills.

2. Knowledge needed

In order to consult, you must have specific expertise usually resulting from an in-depth knowledge of a particular industry, function or technique. You also need a broad business knowledge such as accounting, market and competitor knowledge, and company knowledge. Individuals who have worked for larger organizations often lack this broader business knowledge.

Case study: Frank

Frank has worked for a major computer hardware and software manufacturer for over 20 years. During this time he has been able to attend lots of training programmes, work in many different departments and been able to practise leading edge process reengineering. He has never done any consulting, so he believes the advantages to him are more control over his own destiny, greater potential income and diversity of projects. He knows he has limited knowledge of the consulting process and marketing strategies, but he believes with his network of contacts and his experience he has enough basis to explore consulting as a career choice.

Skills required

Most consultants have a specialized skill set. Successful consultants have all four of the skills in the following major categories:

◆ **Technical/functional skills**. You must have something of particular value to offer the client. This is an area of functional speciality such as marketing, product management, training, computer training, human resources, etc. These are the skills most individuals consider when considering consulting as a career option.

◆ **Communication/interpersonal skills**. This is the ability to convey important information, both in verbal and written form. Ninety per cent of a consultant's day is spent communicating. Without effective communication skills you will have no work. Specific communication skills include presentation skills, listening skills, and negotiating and writing skills. You also need interpersonal skills in order to effectively manage the behaviour of both the client and yourself during the engagement. Many consultants fail because they can do the work, but cannot communicate this ability to different clients.

◆ **Business management skills**. This is the ability to understand the critical elements of running a business, including administration, cash flow, marketing, etc.

◆ **Administrative/organizational skills**. These are the skills necessary for managing projects and paperwork. With no organization structure around you, you will not be successful, e.g. remembering to send a bill is critical!

> **Case study: Julia**
>
> Julia has in-depth human resources (functional) skills originating from her work in employee relations, benefits and compensation, and as a generalist. In addition, Julia is an excellent communicator. She excels at defining the outcome and defining the steps to achieve it in a logical way. Her work at small companies has provided her with a strong business background: as part of the executive team in three start-ups, she was no stranger to financial figures. Finally Julia is very organized – she doesn't go anywhere without her Palm Pilot!

3. Credibility

Clients want to use someone they can trust and therefore need proof of your trustworthiness. You can build credibility both by referring to your background, and from your behaviour when you interact with the client. You can use accomplishments in previous jobs and referrals to build credibility when you are getting started. In addition, companies you have worked for in the past, and job titles you have held, can build your credibility.

> **Time out!**
> Did you know that the number one way to build credibility with clients is Do What You Say You Will Do (DWYSYWD for short)?

Your curriculum vitae (CV) can provide information on proven knowledge skills or experience. In some consulting areas specific qualifications can be used to establish credibility e.g. certification in a certain methodology. You also build credibility by doing what you say you will do: if you say you will send information, do it. If you can't, call and explain why and try to negotiate a new deadline.

4. Personality

Consultants tend to be self-starters, with high energy levels, a high degree of self-confidence and a high tolerance for ambiguity. They need to be curious and creative in order to help clients solve problems. Other personality traits we have heard described by clients are self-discipline, perseverance, empathy, tenacity and detail orientation. Consultants must also be independent, assertive and tenacious. With no set pattern of work, and no formal performance evaluation process, a consultant has to be strongly self-directed. A sense of humour is also a big help.

> **Time out!**
> Did you know that, according to the Barclay's Bank Small Business Characteristics, the following personality attributes were the top three for success?
> ◆   90% were able to get on with customers and staff
> ◆   88% were highly motivated
> ◆   84% were resilient – able to bounce back after problems.

5. Networking

Consulting is a relationship sell. To survive as a consultant, you need to create personal and professional networks. These provide both a marketing base as well as a source of support and are critical for building an on-going practice. You also need a network of fellow consultants to provide help with specific large projects or fill in for you when necessary. As your network is such a key business development tool, more detail about networking is included in Chapter Five.

Case study: Joe

Joe's number one strength is his network. He tends to be gregarious, social and energetic, with a fantastic sense of fun. Customers, team members and friends gravitate towards him because of his positive outlook and are always looking out for opportunities to work with him.

6. A code of ethics

Word travels fast. You are only as successful as your reputation is clear. A code of ethics can help you in guiding your decisions on what work to take or not take, and normally reflects things such as customer focus, regular examination of the consulting practice and open attitudes towards a variety of people.

Foul!

Remember even if you are desperate for money starting out, don't take work for which you are not really qualified. If you cannot deliver to a sufficient standard it will be damaging to your credibility. Better by far to find someone else who can do the work. Ultimately you get more work because what goes around comes around!

7. Lifestyles

A consultant's lifestyle may involve travel, long hours and pressure. The benefits balancing this are a high degree of autonomy, the chance to help and influence others, and the possibility of high earnings, status and respect. Too many consultants are not prepared, nor do they have the support structure for this lifestyle. It is important that your significant others understand the complexity of the process, realizing that a day working at home is not a day off, and that working at home is still working! Building a support structure of other consultants in the business will give you someone to lean on when the occasional proposal is rejected. Don't kid yourself thinking you'll have lots of time off. You won't!

Case studies

Frank

Frank is recently divorced and has no additional financial responsibilities, so he thinks that this is the best time to try out being a consultant.

Joe

Joe's partner works full time and is supportive of this opportunity for Joe to try out consulting.

Based on these characteristics, it is often helpful to assess the extent to which you possess these qualities. Here is an example of a typical self-assessment:

Category	Your self-assessment
Consulting process awareness	Thorough knowledge of all steps from working for Bain and Company.
Knowledge	Functional knowledge in business process reengineering. Good general business knowledge.
Skills	Excellent written communication skills. May have to work on interpersonal skills with clients – can tend to be too abrupt. Excellent organization and follow-through skills.
Personality	Resourceful and independent minded. Persistent.
Credibility	Over ten years' consulting experience with major multinational organizations.
Ethics	Haven't thought about it – will need to consider prior to taking first assignment.
Network	Strong network but for the organization not for me. Have to investigate non-compete clauses.
Lifestyle	Not married so plenty of freedom. Know several other independent consultants for advice and insight if needed.

Exercise 2.3   Assessing your ability as a consultant

- Take a moment and review the previous categories.
- For each category, objectively assess your ability.
- What are your strengths – how can you capitalize on them?
- What about the areas in which you appeared weaker? How could you supplement your knowledge in each area?
- Complete the table below.
- Share this table with some business and personal friends and see what else they would add.

Category	Your self-assessment
Consulting process awareness	
Knowledge	
Skills	
Personality	
Credibility	
Ethics	
Network	
Lifestyle	

Coaching point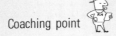

You don't have to be proficient in all areas, you just need to be able to work on your strengths and balance any potential weaknesses.

Of all the categories, probably *consulting process awareness* represents the most important factor to consider because this influences the overall activities of your consulting business.

Consulting and the four temperaments

The unexamined life is not worth living.   *Socrates*

Individuals often use a detailed self-assessment process, such as taking the Myers Briggs Type Indicator (MBTI®) to more fully understand and work with their innate preferences (see Appendix). As a consultant, you are what you sell, so self-knowledge is critical to running a successful business in order to capitalize on your strengths and overcome your weaknesses.

David Keirsey is the synthesizer of modern temperament theory. Using his concepts of temperament will also enable you to more fully understand your innate needs and values. Each of us views the world through our own set of lenses and perceptions, distorting reality to match our own mental picture. We are all unique individuals with our own complexities and idiosyncrasies, but for the 25 centuries since Socrates four basic patterns have been consistently and cross-culturally recognized in the human personality.

Time out!

Temperament theory is based on four sets of themes. These sets serve as fractals of personality. A fractal is 'a pattern underlying seemingly random phenomena'. The human personality is complex and varying, but temperament reveals the underlying inborn foundation on which it is built. In temperament theory, we start with an understanding of the core themes and then examine our basic psychological needs, our core values, our favourite talents, our common approaches and habitual worldview. People with the same temperament share the same core needs and values.

This does not mean that these people are all the same! There are wide varieties, but with strong shared needs. For example, string instruments are a family of musical instruments, but there are huge differences between a guitar and a double bass.

Temperament characteristics

David Keirsey, in *Please Understand Me* and *Please Understand Me II*, selected an animal as a metaphor for each temperament. He believed the innate patterns of behaviour and preferences demonstrated by each animal were somewhat reflective of the characteristics associated with each human temperament.

Exercise 2.4   Animal characteristics

In the space below list four or five things you know about, or associations you have, regarding each of the following animals:

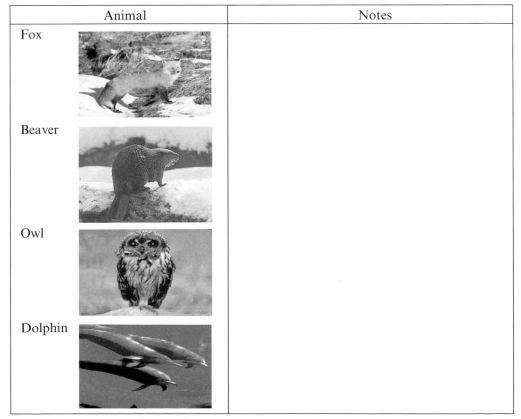

Animal	Notes
Fox	
Beaver	
Owl	
Dolphin	

Adapted from Linda Berens, *The Facilitator's Guide*

In the following chart you'll find an expansion of the list you just started on the general characteristics of the four animals. Explore each set, paying special attention to the major patterns, and keep your own behaviours, needs and values in mind as a point of comparison.

Animals and characteristics

Animal	Characteristics
Fox	◆ appear as fast reacting, quick and resourceful animals ◆ excellent sensory perception: can hear a mouse squeak from up to 100 feet! ◆ leave a scent mark because they want others to know they have been there ◆ alert to the environment – notice any change of movement in the landscape ◆ animals frequently play together ◆ take advantage of opportunities – eat any animal they find and can catch ◆ adaptable – change location easily based on environmental changes or alterations in the food supply ◆ beautiful, well-groomed fur
Beaver	◆ appear as busy, industrious, hard working animals ◆ multi-generational family structure: mate for life, are protective of their family and live in family groups ◆ build strong dams to protect their lodges – specific manner of building keeps water entrances from freezing over in winter ◆ build in a consistent manner and continually enlarge and repair dam and lodge as needed ◆ use large flat tails for packing down materials and slapping the water to warn others of danger ◆ conserving: use all parts of the tree they cut down and stockpile food for winter use ◆ cooperate and rarely fight with other beavers ◆ will change location, but with ample consideration of adequate water, forest and seclusion
Owl	◆ appear as wise and knowledgeable animals ◆ expansive vision: see 100 times better than humans and head rotates almost 360 degrees ◆ big watchful eyes and solemn stance give the appearance of wisdom and composure ◆ scan everything from a high perch then silently swoop down to precisely pick out prey ◆ from their high perch, see things coming in the forest before other animals ◆ anticipate food supply and stagger young accordingly ◆ acute hearing works in a three-dimensional sense – can precisely locate prey in the dark or underneath groundcover ◆ one of the few universal animals: complex varieties are present in every region of the world ◆ independent: will make sure their offspring leave the nest at a young age after receiving the critical teachings
Dolphin	◆ appear as sociable, fun and playful animals ◆ seek interaction with other dolphins and other species ◆ stay with their group – some dolphin species die if separated ◆ advanced communication using complex sounds (phonations) and echolocation ◆ each dolphin and family group has a 'name' which is specific and unique to them ◆ aid the pregnant and injured of their own species and have a 'healing' quality for those who swim with them ◆ use consensus decision-making to change direction ◆ practise hunting skills as play and aid each other against predators ◆ use nose to nudge and guide, but can use it to kill a shark if attacked

Exercise 2.5  Choosing a mascot

Which animal do you most identify with? What were the characteristics that most appealed to you and why? Write your answers in the appropriate box.

Fox ☐	Beaver ☐	Owl ☐	Dolphin ☐

Coaching point

Every person will have elements of all four temperaments. What is useful to identify is the most important driving forces for you as an individual. This will tend to influence what you enjoy about consulting and your ultimate success at it.

These animal 'mascots' correspond to the four temperament names we will be using in the following ways:

Fox: the Artisan temperament	**Owl: the Rational temperament**
Driven by the need to respond in the moment; free-thinking and adaptable, Artisans like to live one day at a time, seizing the day and all the freedom they can get. They are the natural crisis managers and performers. Words to describe Artisans' roles as consultants have included tacticians, trouble-shooters, fire-fighters and negotiators.	Driven by the need for knowledge and competence; big picture focused and independent, Rationals seek to understand the operating principles of all around them and create their own destiny. Words to describe Rationals' roles in consulting have included strategists, marketing, design and systems analysts.

Beaver: the Guardian temperament	Dolphin: the Idealist temperament
Driven by the need to be responsible, build results and be part of a team, Guardians wish to serve and protect those close to them. Words to describe Guardians' roles in consulting have included process improvement, statistical process control, reengineering and quality management.	Driven by the need to have a purpose; relationship-focused and empathetic, Idealists are soul-searchers who constantly quest for meaning and significance in their lives. Words to describe Idealists' roles in consulting have included coaches, catalysts, advocates and facilitators.

As we take a closer look at the characteristics of each temperament, the symbolic meaning of each mascot will become increasingly clear. Once we understand our own basic patterns, it becomes much easier to make more effective choices and communicate with those who are different from us. Let's look at these temperaments in more detail (see page 31).

Now that you have reviewed the characteristics of each temperament, use the following exercise to explore yourself to see which temperament you most gravitate towards.

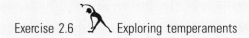

Exercise 2.6   Exploring temperaments

In the space below, within each box:

◆ Write your name in what you perceive to be your 'best-fit' temperament box with the characteristics of that temperament with which you most associate.

◆ You may also be gravitating towards a second temperament: write your name in that box, also with the characteristics of that temperament with which you associate.

◆ Read the case studies for further clarification. You can also read more about temperament at keirsey.com.

Artisan	Rational
Guardian	Idealist

Characteristics of each temperament

Characteristics	Artisan	Guardian	Rational	Idealist
Estimated percentage of world population	Approximately 40%	Approximately 40%	Approximately 10%	Approximately 10%
Driving forces/core needs	Be noticed or make an impact Get a result Act swiftly and practically in the moment	Act responsibly and dutifully Be part of a group or team Contribute to a concrete goal or accomplishment	Demonstrate knowledge and competence Be an expert Retain autonomy and control in activities	Have a greater purpose and meaning for actions Develop their own and others' potential Seek unique identity
Myers Briggs Type Indicator (MBTI) letters	SP	SJ	NT	NF
Work approach	Seek to make an impact with their style and skills Tactical trouble-shooters and fire-fighters	Get the right thing to the right place, in the right quantity at the right price at the right time Put in repeatable processes	Logical, independent, strategic thinkers Driven to improve systems and redesign processes	Build bridges between groups Provide connection and enthusiasm
Time preference/focus	The present: here and now	The past: what was done before	The future: infinite time orientation	The future: life's a journey forward
Communication style	Net it out/get to the point Concise communication – less is more	Linear and sequential: 1,1a, 1b, 2, 2a, 2a.1 etc. Structured: beginning, middle, end	Abstract around models Uses critical questioning	Empathetic Flowing and effusive
Language	Informal/casual with occasional slang Creatively and humorously economical	Respectful and appropriate to the group Conventional	Precise and articulate Avoids redundancy	Generalizations and impressionistic Employ hyperbole
Favourite Words/ Expressions	Fun Excitement Challenge	'Do you remember when?' 'What's your experience?' Comparisons, better than/worse than	Why? Conditionals: 'If X, then Y.' Relevant facts and data	Integrate Connection Meaning
What appeals as a consultant	Flexibility Solve tactical problems See tangible results Challenge Excitement and stimulation	Make a contribution See tangible results Structure Improve a process Security/stability	Intellectual stimulation Improve a system Leading edge Opportunity for independent thought Challenge	Contribute to the overall goal Make a difference Genuine relationships Theories that can be related to people Being special
Examples	Winston Churchill, JFK, Larry Ellison, Michael Jordan, Barbara Streisand	Queen Elizabeth, Colin Powell, John Rockefeller, Mother Theresa, Barbara Walters	Margaret Thatcher, Thomas Jefferson, Bill Gates, Ayn Rand, Cybill Shepherd	Gandhi, Martin Luther King, Walt Disney, Ann Morrow Lindbergh, Jane Fonda
Quote	*The right man is the one who seizes the moment* Johann Wolfgang Von Goethe	*The buck stops here* Harry Truman	*I do not think much of a man who is not wiser today than he was yesterday* Abraham Lincoln	*Happiness is when what you think and what you say and what you do are in harmony* Mahatma Gandhi
Gift to the world	Making the best of the present moment	Bringing the best of the past to the future	Designing a better future	Bringing hope for a better future

◆ Based on what you have chosen: what would be your strengths as a consultant? What do you need in order to succeed? What might be your potential challenges?

Strengths	Potential challenges

Coaching points

◆ If you see yourself in one of these temperament patterns, you are in the right place – great! Keep learning about it and others. Think about what that means in terms of your actions and interactions.

◆ If you see yourself in more than one temperament, don't feel lost. Most of us see a bit of ourselves in all four groupings. Don't feel that temperament is a box you are being stuffed into. We are complex beings and these categories represent a simplified set of similarities. These are patterns to identify with and in no way will be able to completely define you.

Case studies: temperament as consultants

Joe is an Artisan. He enjoys hands-on, fast-paced work that produces concrete results. One of his greatest highs is in seeing a new product successfully launched. He enjoys multiplexing between different tasks and his greatest challenge at work is getting bored because the work is tending to get repetitive. He is great at picking up opportunities in the moment, and this has contributed to him being very successful at product launches. (His MBTI® type is ESFP – one of the four versions of Artisans.)

Frank is a Guardian. He enjoys working in a team, and contributing to concrete results. He naturally establishes structure, organization and processes and uses his sequential thinking innately in his process reengineering work. He enjoys managing projects because there is a beginning, middle and end, and will pride himself on living up to his responsibilities. (His MBTI type is ESTJ – one of the four versions of Guardians.)

Julia is a Rational. She enjoys starting with the big picture and using logical thinking to achieve a long-term goal. She enjoys the independence and autonomy that her role in HR provides and particularly enjoys working with the executive team on strategic analysis and direction. She enjoys creating a model for human resource practices but tends to want to move on when the work becomes more routine. (Her MBTI® type is INTJ – one of the four versions of Rationals.)

Marie is an Idealist. She enjoys working in the training and development field because this innately focuses on developing people's abilities and potential. She enjoys meeting and interacting with a variety of people, and can normally find connections with others. Her empathy allows people to open up to her and enables her to assess clients' needs. (Her MBTI® type is ENFJ – one of the four versions of Idealists.)

So do people enjoy being self-employed?

Going to work for a large company is like getting on a train: are you going 60 miles per hour or is the train going 60 miles an hour and you're just sitting still?

J. Paul Getty

After considering all the previous factors, disadvantages, the knowledge, skills and personality you need to become a successful consultant, by this point you might be thinking 'Is this worth it?!'

Interestingly enough, research conducted in 2000 by MORI (a major market research agency) into Britain's self-employed, documented in *I Want To Be My Own Boss – Inside the New Self-Employed Revolution*, came up with the following results.

Time out!
◆ 86% said self-employment was more enjoyable than having a permanent job
◆ 85% would take the same decision again to work for themselves
◆ 78% feel they now have a much better quality of life
◆ 65% claim to have more time to do the things they enjoy.
Source: Alodis/MORI poll 2000

So, in order to assess whether consulting is for you, investigate the area in which you wish to consult and consider another few key pointers:

◆ do something you really enjoy
◆ build a network; talk to as many people as you can in the business
◆ set realistic goals
◆ be patient.

Exercise 2.7  Is consulting for you?

Checklist

Spend a few moments reviewing the information and the characteristics described on the previous pages and evaluate how closely you meet those criteria.

◆ Do you fully understand the consulting process?
◆ What are your functional skills or specialized content knowledge?
◆ How do you rate your skills?
◆ How credible are you as a consultant?
◆ Does your personality fit?
◆ Did you have a clearly defined code of ethics?
◆ What is the size of your network?
◆ Does consulting fit your lifestyle?
◆ Can you deliver the work?
◆ Can you market the work?
◆ Can you organize the work?
◆ Can you budget to manage the ups and downs?
◆ Is this work something you really enjoy?

Scorecard

Before moving on to Chapter 3, think about the following questions:

◆ In terms of considering the advantages and disadvantages of consulting as a profession, have you created an objective list of pros and cons of this profession to you? Have you discussed this list with those who are close to you? Have you discussed the list with people who are consultants in your chosen area of practice?

◆ In terms of the qualities of successful consultants, have you evaluated yourself against the critical categories outlined by Kelley? What are your critical competencies? Where do you rate yourself as lacking skills, knowledge or expertise? How can you capitalize on your competencies? How could you build capabilities where you perceive you may be exposed?

◆ Have you completed the exercises on temperament? Have you reviewed the other temperament descriptions so that you are familiar with the differences and complexities of each temperament? What effect do you think your temperament might have on your ability as a consultant?

CHAPTER THREE

What Type of Consulting Business Are You Running?

 Game plan

The first critical stage in starting your own practice is to be specific about your business direction by defining your vision for the future of your consulting business, identifying your unique selling proposition, and categorizing the main responsibilities for your consulting business.

The purpose of this chapter therefore is to help you:

◆ Create a vision for your consulting business to keep you focused on 'bad days'.

◆ More clearly articulate your possible strengths and weaknesses as a consultant.

◆ Clearly define what you can uniquely contribute to the client.

◆ Analyse your business using SWOT analysis.

◆ Build an overview of your business activities so that you can focus on what is important.

Why define your business before jumping in?

Often when individuals consider becoming a consultant, they think of the logistical steps in getting started such as getting business cards, setting up the office, buying a computer, etc. But the first critical stage in starting your own practice is to define what you want your business to 'be'. Most people begin with a vague notion they want to be a consultant but it is very important to become specific.

Foul!

When people describe what they want to do they make two main mistakes:

◆ First, they explain what they want to do in vague, long sentences.

◆ Second, they try to be a 'jack-of-all-trades' and not be tied to one area. Trying to be all things to all people can result in not being anything to anyone!

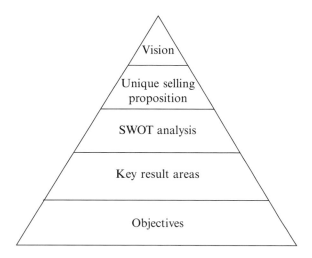

Fig. 3.1. Steps in setting business direction.

Defining your vision

What is a **vision statement**?

True vision is always twofold. It involves emotional comprehension as well as physical perception.

Ross Parmenter

A vision is defined as a picture of future greatness, a definition of core values, and a lighthouse towards the frontier. Your vision must make sense to others, stretch your imagination, give an 'aha' effect, but at the same time be within the bounds of possibility. Your vision statement describes the grand idea of what you are about, the future as you want it to be: 'I am in the business of. . .' The vision statement must be reasonably precise yet still provide a general direction to your consulting business.

Coaching point

While some of these exercises in this section may appear time consuming and not directly linked to deliverables, investing in this area will produce long term benefits for you and your consulting business through greater focus and raised motivation.

The vision statement tends to be abstract, high level, without much concrete detail. It has also been compared to the North Star: high above, constantly present, universally known, guiding direction. The purpose of your vision statement is to guide your decision-making, provide a yardstick to keep you on track and provide inspiration in achieving your goals.

Examples of vision statements

Examples of vision statements from organizations are:

Oracle: *To enable the Information Age through network computing.*

Kepner Tregoe: *We focus on the human side of change through providing skills development programs and consulting services.*

Raychem: *To win the respect of our Customers around the world by being a leader in delivering innovative solutions.*

Case study: Frank's vision

Frank defined his vision as 'To help call centres optimize their productivity'. He believed this provided a good overall direction, but that it did not limit him to only process reengineering. Key words in his vision statement were 'call centres' (this could include technical support and customer service centres), 'optimize', 'productivity'. He wanted to ensure that any work he conducted would have a tangible bottom line effect on the company. 'If it did not make a difference at 9 on a Monday morning, he would not have succeeded.'

Differentiating between vision and mission statements

A **mission statement** communicates the vision by considering several critical variables:

◆ What is it that the organization wants to do?

◆ Who is the organization's customer?

- What are our values?
- What profit do we need to make?

When you are getting started in your consulting business, using a vision statement alone, with **key result areas** is probably adequate. Adding another level of detail may make the process too complex.

Creating your vision statement

Time out!
A man was passing a work site and saw three bricklayers. He approached the first bricklayer and asked 'What are you doing?' The man answered, 'Making a living.' He asked the second man the same question and he answered, 'Laying bricks.' He asked the third worker the same question and the man responded, 'Building a Cathedral.' A strong vision statement enables you to feel as though you are building a cathedral, not just laying bricks or making a living.

Exercise 3.1  Defining your vision statement

- Take a moment and think about the following questions:
  - Why do you want to be a consultant?
  - What is it that you primarily want to achieve?
  - What do you want your customers to achieve using your services?
  - What is your ultimate theme?
  - What is the reason your consulting business was created?
  - What would success look like for you?
  - Think of an ideal day: what would you do? Who would you work with?
    Where would you work? What would be the result?
  - Think of some times you felt really motivated: what were you doing? With whom?
  - What made it motivational for you?

- Now try to write your vision statement in the space below:

  Helping peace workers and organise them to optimize their impact *activish*

My vision statement is:

_____

_____

_____

_____

◆ Now check your vision statement using the following questions.

Yes No

☐ ☐ Does your vision statement energize you?

☐ ☐ Does your vision statement reflect all the services you could provide?

☐ ☐ Can you remember your vision statement without referring to a written version?

◆ Share your answers with friends and consultants to get feedback.

◆ Now integrate these ideas to create a more focused vision statement. Make sure it answers the earlier questions and that it consists of less than nine words to ensure that it is easy to remember.

My vision statement is:

_____

_____

_____

_____

Coaching point

Creating a vision statement will take you some time to complete. Often the first ideas you come up with tend to be more detail oriented. If this is the case you will need to continue refining the statement by talking to friends, professional acquaintances and prospective customers. Time invested in this area will reap rewards for your business in the long term.

Case study: Marie

Marie defined her vision as 'To provide consulting services to allow individuals and teams to maximize results'. Although the statement is a little long, she believes the vision encompasses the critical direction of her business: the key words are 'consulting', and 'individuals', 'teams', and 'results'. She would have preferred to say 'develop their potential' but she thinks that these words might not be acceptable in the business community.

Common challenges that arise in trying to define a vision include being too specific, too 'pie in the sky', not able to share with customers, or appearing as if they are not related to business objectives.

Defining strengths and weaknesses

Now that we have identified our vision, we need to define what we 'bring to the table' to aid our clients; our **unique selling proposition**. The first step in this process is to be able to objectively define our strengths and competencies. Many are natural to us and therefore we do not think about them, but in order to capitalize on our strengths we need to be aware of them.

> This above all; to thine own self be true.
>
> *William Shakespeare*

When we raised the topic of self-knowledge while working with a 50-year-old client from IBM, he questioned 'Do you honestly think people reach the age of 50 without knowing themselves?' Our answer: 'Absolutely!' Understanding what is important to us and how we operate is not necessarily as obvious as you might think. Looking inside and trying to sort out the collage of abilities, skills, strengths and weaknesses that make up our personality can be quite a challenge.

Consider the complexity of developing an accurate perception of your own strengths and weaknesses. In the strengths and weaknesses window below, there are four quadrants.

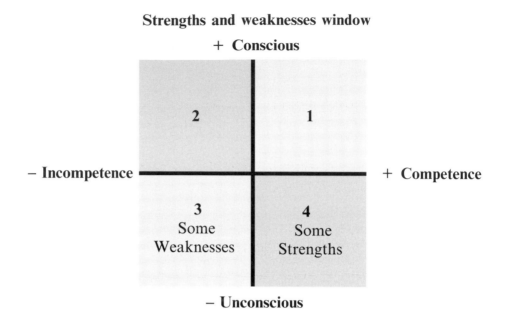

Strengths and weaknesses window

Fig. 3.2. Conscious and unconscious competence.

- Quadrant 1: **Conscious competence**: We are aware of certain talents, skills and abilities.

- Quadrant 2: **Conscious incompetence**. We are also painfully aware of some of our weaknesses, blind spots, and shortcomings.

However, there are also two other quadrants that others may see, but that we are not tuned into.

- Quadrant 3: **Unconscious incompetence**. These include our most plaguing weaknesses. We don't know, but we don't know that we don't know!

- Quadrant 4: **Unconscious competence**: These are some of our key strengths, although we take them for granted because they are natural to us. We know, but we don't know that we know!

How you see yourself can vary significantly from how others see you. The implications of this possible lack of self-knowledge on your business performance are considerable. You might think you were communicating clearly, but the client could have no idea what you were talking about!

I have had more trouble with myself than with any other man I have met.

Dwight L. Moody

Exercise 3.2 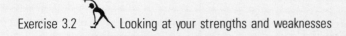 Looking at your strengths and weaknesses

Use the blank strengths and weaknesses window that follows to self-assess your innate abilities, skills and aptitudes by quadrant.

◆ **Quadrant 1: Conscious competence**. Think about a significant work achievement. What was that achievement? What made this an important success for you? What did you uniquely say or do that contributed to this achievement? What did you do here that was different from what others might have done? What was it that you were able to uniquely contribute to the success of this project? What strengths might have enabled your accomplishment? Try to list at least three specific strengths in quadrant 1.

◆ **Quadrant 2: Conscious incompetence**. Think about a work task that was not as successful as you wished it to be. Why was it a disappointment? What did you specifically say or do that might have contributed to this occurrence? What possible weaknesses can you infer from your analysis? List them in quadrant 2.

◆ **Quadrant 3: Unconscious incompetence**. Talk to three people whom you like and respect. Ask them for their honest feedback on what they perceive to be your greatest weakness or challenge. List at least one challenge in quadrant 3 that they mention, but that you *did not* note in quadrant 2.

◆ **Quadrant 4: Unconscious competence**. Ask the same individuals what attributes, characteristics or competencies they value most about you. List at least three strengths in quadrant 4 that they observe, but that you *did not* note in quadrant 1.

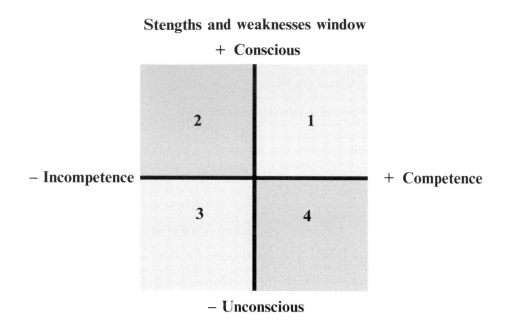

Fig. 3.3. Your strengths and weaknesses.

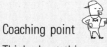
Coaching point

Think about this exercise using these questions:

◆ What did you learn about your possible strengths from this exercise?

◆ What did you learn about your possible challenges from this exercise?

◆ What implications could this learning have for understanding your abilities as a consultant?

Identifying your unique selling proposition

Your **unique selling proposition** is how you define your specific contribution within your chosen area of expertise. It identifies why someone should buy your services and not someone else's. It is a statement reflecting your competitive advantage.

Exercise 3.3. Defining your unique selling proposition

Now that you have identified both your areas of conscious competence (known strengths) and unconscious competence (innate strengths), think about what this means to your clients in terms of what you can bring to the table that others can't.

Example:
A director of training at a retail company had rolled out a sales training programme to over 200 retail stores, resulting in a 16% comparative store sales increase. The company had tried to roll out a sales training programme two years previously and it had not worked. When he asked the question 'What did he do that the previous director of training had not done?' he identified the following factors that had uniquely contributed to the programme's success.
◆ He had obtained senior management commitment.
◆ He had involved the retail team in the development of the programme.
◆ He had simplified the design of the content.
◆ He had ensured there were follow-up strategies in place to ensure continuity of change.
From this he deduced that part of his unique selling proposition was his ability to accurately identify customer needs, tailor an appropriate solution to customer needs and thereby to ensure solutions were commercially viable.

Please spend a few moments and identify critical components in your unique selling proposition.

_____

_____

_____

_____

Coaching point
Asking friends, previous employers and professional peers for their insight can provide other useful data in documenting your unique selling proposition. Often it is hard for us to identify our positive characteristics.

Your unique selling proposition has both an internal and an external focus. For instance a trainer might claim her unique selling proposition (with an internal focus to her business) is that she has excellent facilitation skills. The unique selling proposition from the customer's perspective (the external focus) is that she has the ability to motivate small and large groups.

Case Study: Julia

Julia's unique selling proposition is that she is a business-focused, strategic human resources partner. She specializes in integrating human resources policies with business requirements to minimize risk and legal liability. She refined this understanding by talking to previous employers and colleagues and asking them to explain what they valued about her insights. They told her that unlike many HR professionals who tend to talk about rules and structure, she linked this knowledge to business issues and needs.

Your vision and unique selling proposition are valuable, in terms of the direction they provide to your business, but also in terms of their use in marketing your services. While the process of defining them is difficult, they are a critical step in your journey to create your own successful consulting business. Make sure you continue working on your vision and unique selling proposition until they are accurate.

SWOT analysis

What is success? I think it is a mixture of having a flair for the thing that you are doing; knowing that it is not enough, that you have got to have hard work and a certain sense of purpose.

Margaret Thatcher

SWOT analysis means taking a probing look at the strengths, weaknesses, opportunities and threats that face your consulting business. The analysis is a process of investigating and brainstorming the factors working for and against your practice that could affect overall performance.

Time out!

Strengths and *weaknesses* refer to your business's internal advantages and potential disadvantages. These factors are in your direct control. *Opportunities* and *threats* allude to aspects outside of your direct control that might open up potential (opportunities) or result in negative consequences (threats). Opportunities and threats can both originate in the market at large or from other consulting organizations.

The purpose of SWOT analysis is to view the world in which you are performing from a macro perspective. This vantage point ensures that the planned strategy and direction are possible, given your inherent strengths and weaknesses. It also assures that the strategy is geared towards capitalizing on opportunities and minimizing threats.

Case study: Joe's SWOT analysis

Joe's SWOT analysis included the following data:

Strengths	Weaknesses
20 years' experience	Lack of administrative support
Excellent network of contacts	Lack of procedures
Great background in successfully launching products	Limited financial resources
	Too broad a focus
Great marketing skills	Dislike of doing the mundane part of project management
Package of services available to sell	
Action oriented	
Opportunities	**Threats**
Thriving market	Many one-person and larger consulting firms
Companies are downsizing so there is more demand for outsourcing services	Future financial market stability
Product marketing has proven business results	Difficulty in raising market awareness
Many business publications talk about the speed of product release being critical to business success	Difficulty in clearly identifying the advantage in his services

Exercise 3.4   Conducting SWOT analysis for your business

♦ Spend some time individually brainstorming what you perceive to be the strengths and possible weaknesses of your consulting business. Use the ideas listed in the conscious and unconscious competence grid to further supplement your ideas.

♦ Then consider the market you are targeting for your services. Spend a few moments listing opportunities and threats of which you are aware. Take the opportunity to talk to other people in the same market segment, friends, colleagues, other consultants, etc. (See Chapter 5 for more detail on market research strategies.) List the associated opportunities and threats in the grid below.

Strengths	Weaknesses
Opportunities	**Threats**

♦ Thinking about your strengths and weaknesses, what would you have to do to capitalize on your strengths and minimize your weaknesses to optimize your consulting business results?

_____

_____

♦ Considering the current business climate, what can you do to take advantage of opportunities and minimize the risks associated with the threats?

_____

_____

Coaching point

Conducting a SWOT analysis is great when you start your business, but is also useful once a year to keep a pulse on your business opportunities.

Case study: Frank

Frank believed that working for large organizations was where he could add the most value. He thought his unique selling proposition was 'A technically competent engineer who can accurately improve call centre operations'. He believed many engineers, while they possessed the technical skills to undertake process reengineering, lacked the interpersonal skills required to build relationships, and be a successful consultant. In his SWOT analysis he identified as opportunities the huge growth in call centres, but highlighted as a possible weakness/threat the challenges of being a small player in such a huge unregulated market. He realized he would have to use creative marketing channels to be able to successfully launch his business.

Establishing key result areas

Now that you have established your overall direction, it is important to define your essential business responsibilities.

If a man knows not what harbour he seeks, any wind is the right wind.

Seneca

Linking what to when

While many consultants set objectives for their business often there is no direct link between the business's vision/unique selling proposition and the tasks that have to be completed on a day-to-day basis. In fact, often you have what appears to be a never-ending list of projects, while what you do day-to-day is not represented at all. As a result you appear as though you are not performing and become overloaded and stressed.

Time out!

Key result areas reflect the most important areas of your consulting business responsibilities, the areas in which results have to be achieved. You need to concentrate your time and resources in these sectors in order to accomplish your goals. Establishing key result areas is a valuable technique that links the overall direction of your consulting practice with project goals and milestones.

Guidelines for defining key result areas

Key result areas do *not* describe the type of results to be achieved, but rather categorize work into *headings*. This grouping procedure is a valuable tool for consultants as the process complements the way the human brain naturally works.

Time out!

Overview and the brain:

Did you know that...?

◆ The *subconscious brain* works 24 hours a day and has, as far as we know, unlimited capacity.

◆ We also have a *conscious brain*, which works only when we are awake and can concentrate on one thought at a time. As a result, when we have a multitude of tasks to complete we may feel overloaded.

◆ The *preconscious brain* reduces this perceived overload because it can keep an outline or overview of seven +/- two, i.e., five to nine categories.

We now need to group all the tasks we need to complete under no more than nine headings in order to be able to build an overview of overall workload: the key result areas. This process also gives a feeling of control and can reduce stress.

Guidelines for defining key result areas

Be brief	Use a maximum of one to four words for your key result area titles. Example: financial management.
Headings	Key result areas should be headings that describe areas within which team results are to be achieved. They should not state specific aims or performance standards. Example: 'customer satisfaction' would be a key result area not 'increase customer satisfaction scores by ... %'.
Complete	Key result areas should cover *all* aspects of your business – all you do and ought to do needs to be included somewhere in a key result area.
Clear	Key result areas should be immediately understandable to yourself and others. Example: 'problem identification' might be too vague: what problems?
Avoid overlapping	When two key result areas are just different aspects of the same subject, they should be combined into one topic. Example: 'marketing communications' and 'advertising' could be combined under 'marketing management.'
Scope	Your key result areas should not extend beyond your sphere of responsibility.

Case study: Joe's key result areas

Key result area	Explanation
Target companies/clients	This section will include specific companies that are targeted as specific clients. When the first client is closed and paid for (see section two), this key result area will become current clients.

Business development	This section includes activities such as his sales phone calls, e-mails, proposals, sales appointments and contracts. It involves everything from the time the lead surfaces as a prospect to the time he begins the actual work. See Chapter 6 for more specifics.
Marketing activities	This section includes activities such as conducting market research, advertising, PR, creating flyers, distributing newsletters, etc. This reflects the more indirect building of market awareness and client interest. See Chapter 5 for more specifics.
Product development	This section includes defining and developing the range of products and services. Joe needs to more clearly define his product offering in terms of the benefits to customers and the specific features that are provided. See Chapter 5 for more specifics.
Organization/planning	Joe is very aware that planning is not his strong suit. This section includes a month by month action plan. See Chapter 10 for more information.
Financial management	This area includes invoicing, cash management, credit collection and forward budgeting. See Chapter 7 for more specifics.
Networking	Joe believes at this early stage that his network is so important that he wants to keep it as a separate key result area to remind him to invest time and energy in this area every week. See Chapter 5.
Professional development	Joe wants to ensure he does not neglect his own development so he has established a key result area to highlight this aspect of his time management.

Key result areas

> He who wants to do everything will never do anything.
>
> *André Maurois*

Productivity means accomplishing goals and achieving results. If you are to achieve your overall goals, you need to clearly visualize them and spend your time on the right things, your key result areas. Highly productive consultants carefully focus their planning and management of activities around key result areas. They *choose* to make these a constant priority and manage other responsibilities *after* these key areas are taken care of.

Examples of key results areas:

- finance
- sales
- marketing
- team development
- customer service
- operations
- communication
- reporting
- problem identification.
- projects
- quality
- research and development
- manufacturing
- vendor management
- purchasing
- process improvement
- project management

Establishing your key result areas

Now that we have reviewed the principles inherent in defining key result areas and provided an example, it is time to define your key result areas.

Exercise 3.5   Defining your key result areas

- Individually list the projects/tasks and activities you have on your to-do list onto Post-It® notes.

- Write one specific task or activity on each Post-It® note.

- In addition, you can ask yourself the following questions:
  – Where do I need to pay attention in order to keep an edge on my business?

– What results am I expected to achieve?

– What activities bring the best return?

– How do I spend my time?

– In which areas can I work to create specific results for my company and/or myself?

– What will create the future for my consulting business?

◆ When you cannot think of any more tasks or activities, start moving the Post-It® notes together if they seem to relate to similar things until you have no more than nine categories, but you could include as few as five. For instance, generating invoices and collecting receivables would be placed next to each other.

◆ Think about a heading that would describe each group; this heading will be the name of the key result area.

Example

For instance you might have ideas like:

◆ brainstorm list of contacts

◆ write business plan

◆ do market research

◆ define product/service

◆ talk to people who said they would help me out

◆ do a budget

◆ get a computer

◆ get software

These tasks could be grouped under different headings:

Marketing

◆ do market research

◆ define product/service

Networking

◆ brainstorm list of contacts

◆ talk to people who said they would help me out

Administration/set up
- get a computer
- get software

Financial control
- write business plan
- do a budget

- Transfer your key result areas list to the form below.

Blank key result area form

Key result area	Description

Sample key result areas

Below are the key result areas for most consulting businesses.

MY KEY RESULT AREAS
1 Financial control
2 Clients   A.   B.
3 Business development
4 Database management/marketing
5 Product development
6 Operational effectiveness/administration
7 Team development
8 Professional development

Coaching point

It is important that the words in the key result areas are yours – so that you know where you would 'file' information.

Checklist

1. Have you created an initial vision statement?

2. Did you identify your strengths, both your areas of unconscious and conscious competence?

3. Have you identified your unique selling proposition?

4. Have you listed three people who could give you advice on your vision and unique selling proposition?

5. Have you conducted an initial SWOT analysis for your business?

6. Have you defined the key result areas for your business?

Scorecard

Before moving on to Chapter 4, think about the following questions:

◆ As you define your vision and unique selling proposition, who else can you talk to in order to obtain feedback? What other resources could you use to give you examples and ideas? By what date do you wish to finalize your vision and unique selling proposition? To what extent is there a business focus in your vision and unique selling proposition?

◆ As you conducted your SWOT analysis, what specific threats or weaknesses did you find which might inhibit the future performance of your consulting business? What specific strengths and opportunities did you identify that would help you to build your consulting business? What plans have you put in place to ensure you follow through with your initial ideas?

◆ As you define your key result areas, are they representative of your entire workload? Do the headings make sense and provide you with an accurate overview of your workload? Are they in alignment with your vision and unique selling proposition?

CHAPTER FOUR

Establishing Your Business Direction

Game plan

Once you have established your vision, unique selling proposition, conducted your SWOT analysis and defined the key result areas for your consulting business, it is critical to write in more detail what you specifically wish to accomplish.

The purpose of this chapter therefore is to help you:

◆ Build a business plan.
◆ Decide the optimal legal structure with which to begin your consulting business.
◆ Set objectives for your practice.
◆ Establish preliminary milestones.

Writing a business plan

If you don't know where you are going, you will probably end up somewhere else.

Laurence J. Peter

Time out!

The business plan performs several major functions:

◆ It forces you to think through each aspect of your business while keeping you focused and structured. It also helps set limits.
◆ It provides a yardstick by which you can measure output and success.
◆ It allows a dry run before you actually perform your first consulting assignment, i.e. it exposes you to potential sales, profits and problems.
◆ The business plan becomes a sales tool for both you and your potential investors.

Business plans vary in length and nature and basically comprise of several main sections. For in-depth discussion of business plans, *New Venture Creation and Business Plan Guides at DTI* (www.dti.gov.uk) provide excellent details. Generally, a business plan should be from two to four pages. It should be a good guide, but not so complex that you don't want to change it, because it *will* change.

Writing a business plan

Sections of a typical business plan will include:

General information

Cover page	Name of company, address, phone, date, period covered, name of person who created the plan.
Introductory summary	This is a summary of the important information included in your business plan. Write the summary after you have written the entire plan. Investors often read the introductory summary and decide, based on this section alone, whether to read the rest of the business plan, when deciding whether to contribute funds to the venture.
Table of contents	This lets the reader know what is included in your business plan.

Your company overview

Vision statement	As you defined in Chapter 3: your ultimate purpose or theme.
Unique selling proposition	As you defined in Chapter 3: what you can uniquely contribute to a client.
SWOT analysis	A seasoned businessperson realizes that every venture entails risks. What are the possibilities of competitive responses to your actions? Are there unfavourable trends in the industry? Use the SWOT analysis to help you calculate your risks (also described in Chapter 3). ◆ strengths for your business (internal) ◆ weaknesses for your business (internal) ◆ opportunity in the marketplace (external) ◆ threats in the marketplace (external)

Key result area: finance
(See Chapter 7 for more information.)

Financial plan	Your financial plan identifies the sources and uses of your money in your business. It shows your financial standing through two basic documents: the profit and loss forecasts and the cash flow statements.
Financial funding	After determining how much money you need through your profit and loss and cash flow, your business plan needs to indicate where the money will come from.

Key result area: marketing
(See Chapter 5 for more information.)

Market research	This is a crucial section in the business plan. Many consultants enamoured of their own good idea fail to investigate whether there is a market for it.
Market analysis	In your market analysis you identify your expected major clients, estimate your potential annual sales to each and assess your potential market share. While this market assessment may be to a large extent theoretical in the early stages, it none the less serves to focus and direct your energies.
Marketing plan	The marketing plan gives a picture of the market, your marketing goals, promotional strategies, the definition of your products and services, who the competition is, what you will charge for your services and how to obtain customers.

Key result area: business development

Target clients	To reach your estimated sales projections you must develop a strategy that targets specific clients with specific sales approaches and determine which aspects of your firm's services you will stress in your marketing efforts.

Key result area: organization structure

Management team	The management team is responsible for making your business successful. If you are a solo practitioner, then you are the management team and perform all the major tasks for planning, marketing, accounting, financing, organizing and consulting. The business plan needs to include an overview of your credentials including major accomplishments, degrees, and any other information that will position you as an expert in your field.
Professional assistance	You should quickly establish relationships with necessary professionals such as a lawyer, an accountant, a banker and an insurance agent. Capable professionals provide significant part-time assistance when you are a sole practitioner.
Other resources	You should develop a team of other consultants, e.g. technical writers, editors, trainers, etc to have on hand when you need help with projects. You may also get work from them when they need help.

Key result area: professional development

Research and development	Research and development appears in many forms and has costs associated with it. It can include such things as researching training materials, implementing process improvements, attending conferences to gather current data or developing new services to meet clients' needs.

Overall schedule

Plan	Your schedule pinpoints the timing and interrelationships of all the major events important to starting and developing your business. Some people use flow charts to visualize the process of starting, operating and planning for a growing business. It should also include your tasks and milestones.

Of over 1,000 small firms in 1996, those that had strategic plans had 50% more revenue and profit growth than companies that didn't have one.

Source: www.businessplans.co.uk

Exercise 4.1 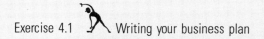 Writing your business plan

♦ Take a moment and think about the sections in the business plan and complete the answers, as far as possible, to the questions below.

General information

Cover page	What will be the name of your company, address, phone, fax, e-mail information etc? When do you want this business plan to be completed? Will you obtain any help in writing the business plan?
Introductory summary	Remember – complete this last! When you look at your business, what is the key data that you want to share with clients? Investors? What captures the essence of the business?
Table of contents	This lets the reader know what is included in your business plan.

Your company overview

Vision statement	Have you defined your vision statement? If not, refer to Exercise 3.1 in Chapter 3.
Unique selling proposition	Have you completed Exercise 3.3? If so complete the answer here.
SWOT analysis	Have you completed Exercise 3.4? What are the key strengths you wish to capitalize on? What opportunities do you wish to exploit with your business? What key risks do you wish to avoid?

Key result area: finance

(See Chapter 7 for more information.)

Financial plan	What are your estimated incomings (see Exercise 7.3)?
	What do you see to be your initial set-up costs (see Exercise 7.1)?
	What do you perceive to be your ongoing expenses (see Exercise 7.1)?
	Include a simple cash flow statement (see Exercise 7.3).
Financial funding	How much cash do you have behind you?
	What are your other resources to deal with financial demands?
	Credit cards, etc (see Exercise 7.2)?

Key result area: marketing

Market research	What market research have you completed (see Exercise 5.1)?
Market analysis	What is it that makes you think there is a market for your product?
	Who else is doing business in the market place?
Marketing plan	What are your marketing goals (see Exercise 5.2)?
	What is your product definition (see Exercise 5.4)?
	How are you going to price your product (see Exercise 7.5)?
	How are you going to distribute your product by the use of your network (see Exercise 5.6)?
	How are you going to promote your product to the market place (see Exercise 5.5)?

Key result area: business development

Target clients	Name three clients who could benefit from your services.

Key result area: organization structure

Management team	Have you completed a CV that captures your key talents?
	Why would investors/customers think you were qualified to help them?
Professional assistance	Who will be your accountant?
	Who will be your lawyer?
	Who else might you need?
Other resources	Who else do you know who you could involve on certain projects if you needed it?

Key result area: professional development

Research and development	How do you plan to stay current in your field? What are the best ways to stay abreast of business developments in your market segment?

Overall schedule

Plan	Have you created a high-level three month plan? A six-month outline? Yearly targets?

◆ Now share your business plan with some others for feedback. What changes would they recommend?

◆ Now check your business plan using the following questions:

Yes No

☐ ☐ Does your business plan succinctly explain your business?

☐ ☐ Is your business plan comprehensible to others?

☐ ☐ Does your business plan include all the relevant data to explain your overall business direction?

Coaching point

Writing a business plan can seem time consuming and irrelevant. Many consultants want to 'get out there and make it happen' instead of fiddling around with this intangible activity. However, time invested in this area can help prevent mistakes such as loss of focus, unclear allocation of resources, and can actually improve the message when in front of clients.

Case study: Frank

Frank began the process of creating a structured business plan, but he wishes to invest more time in this area to ensure that he is clear on his overall direction. So his top short-term objective is:

◆ Ensure a cohesive strategy by finalizing a business plan by 31 December 200X that will be eight pages in length, including finalized vision and unique selling proposition,

SWOT analysis and key result areas with critical objectives and tactics outlined. Meanwhile, he has begun to create a simple marketing presentation on PowerPoint that covers some of the information in his business plan to make sure that he is coherent and consistent when positioning his business to prospective clients.

Making time to complete the business plan will ensure that you are taking the right steps to build your consulting business and will not get side tracked in other areas.

Deciding your legal structure

> This one step – choosing a goal and sticking to it – changes everything. *Scott Reed*

The most common legal structures for a consulting business are the sole proprietorship/ trader, the partnership and the limited company. The structure you choose will be related to your overall business objectives.

> Did you know that . . .
> – 51% of new businesses are set up as sole trader operations
> – 31% as limited liability companies
> – 18% as partnerships
> according to Barclays 'Starting Up in Business'.

Sole proprietorships/traders

Most consulting businesses are sole traders. Under this arrangement you and your business are one and the same. Mostly, if you use your name as the business name, you do not have to file under the assumed business name status. Your firm's net income is taxable as your personal income. You have an unlimited liability for the debts of your firm.

This type of business organization is simple yet effective as you are starting your consulting business. Even if you want to work with another person, it is often better to begin the cooperation as two sole traders. This gives you an opportunity to try out the working relationship, before formalizing a partnership. Unfortunately, there are a lot more broken partnerships than successful ones!

Partnerships

There are two types of partners, general and limited. General partners control the day-to-day operations of the firm and usually have unlimited liability for the firm's debts. Limited partners, also known as silent partners, exercise no control over daily operations. They typically invest money in return for a share of the firm's profits.

Foul!

Many individuals, who have worked together very successfully in a corporation, fail when they try to work together as partners. There are a variety of reasons for this:

1. When working in an organization, the payment is not dependent on the working relationship. Often partners divide because there is not enough business for both partners: one can generate business, but can't do the work. The other can do the work, but cannot generate business. This creates ill-feeling between them.
2. Working in a formal organization structure, there are defined standards and procedures. Working in a partnership, individuals have to define their own structure and they may approach this process differently.
3. If the partners are not clear when defining roles and responsibilities, it can result in frustration and disappointment between partners because others are not 'doing their job'.
4. Working together, 'on top of each other', is different from working in an organization where there are other individuals present.

So think carefully before you make this large commitment. Lawyers may tend to make more money from partnerships than individuals do!

Limited companies

These are generally legal entities separate and distinct from you as an individual. Most larger businesses are limited companies. This brings several advantages including permanence, continuing despite the death of individual shareholders, and your personal liability is limited to the amount invested in stock. However, limited companies have several disadvantages in that they are typically subject to higher taxes and fees, and the procedures, reports and statements required by the government may become cumbersome. See the later section for more information on the tax advantages and disadvantages of a limited company.

Financial and tax implications for different structures

Sole trader	
Advantages	**Disadvantages**
◆ You can claim direct expenses related to the business such as telephone, heat, light, car, meals, etc. Check with your accountant for specific deductions allowed currently. ◆ You can use personal pension schemes to reduce tax liability. ◆ Often, if you work from home, you reduce travel time and expenses. When you do travel for the client you get these costs reimbursed. ◆ This is the simplest structure when working independently. ◆ Lower administrative overheads. ◆ Taxes can be self-assessed. ◆ Less taxes. ◆ If you are making losses initially you can deduct these against any taxes you are paying on full-time employment.	◆ You are responsible for tracking costs and revenue and filing tax returns bi-annually. ◆ You pay National Insurance Contribution but you are not eligible to claim unemployment benefits. ◆ If you are sick, or have illness in the family, your business may be exposed and you may have inadequate financial resources. ◆ Less credibility as a sole trader (may be perceived that way). ◆ May have to guarantee personal loans because of less 'business presence'. ◆ As a business owner you may be liable for losses and debts.
Partnership	
Advantages	**Disadvantages**
◆ You have someone else to ask difficult questions. ◆ You have someone else who shares tax liability.	◆ Apart from the complexity of deciding separate tax bills there are no disadvantages.
Limited company	
Advantages	**Disadvantages**
◆ There is a limit to corporation tax on profits – check with your accountant for the current limits. ◆ Company pension schemes for 'owner directors' are more generous in terms of tax relief than for an individual. ◆ Advantage can be made of additional business deductions such as company cars, although these are less present now than previously. ◆ Greater credibility associated with being a limited company (possibly). ◆ Banks may be willing to provide a loan without a personal guarantee. ◆ Directors are not personally liable for company losses.	◆ There are more stringent reporting requirements than a sole trader. ◆ Higher taxes. ◆ Taxes cannot be self-assessed – need accounting support.

Case study: Marie

Marie has decided to get started as quickly as possible. She has decided that she is going to stay as a sole trader, in the same way as she did last time that she was independent. She believes this will give her the flexibility in the short term, and then she can decide at a later date if she wishes to become a limited company. She has written a simple business plan following the outline in the materials for her own use only, as she does not want to use external funding to start the business.

Exercise 4.2 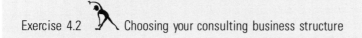 Choosing your consulting business structure

◆ Take a moment and think about the different ways of structuring your business:
sole trader
partnership
limited company.

◆ Review the advantages and possible disadvantages of each structure.

◆ Think about your business, which structure will you select?

_____

_____

◆ What are the advantages of this structure and how will you make sure you benefit from them?

_____

_____

◆ What could be the possible risks associated with that structure and how could you overcome these?

_____

_____

Coaching point

If you are just getting started and are not sure which structure you want to use, begin with sole trader. It requires very little set-up time or administrative overhead, it is legal and you can evaluate this decision later.

Case study: Julia

Even though Julia is just starting up, she has decided to set her business up as a limited liability company because of the area she focuses on: human resources. She wants more legal protection in case she provides advice which then results in a client suing her. Particularly with the sensitivity and possible liability associated with sexual harassment, she feels the increased costs involved will pay for themselves with the additional protection she will possess as a limited liability company.

Setting objectives

If you cry 'Forward,' you must make plain in what direction to go.

Anton Chekhov

Once you have established your key result areas and written your business plan, it is critical to write objectives for your business, and create a list of milestones to ensure you make progress.

What is an objective?

Objectives are concrete, tangible, measurable results or outcomes from your efforts that you can see, not just roles or activities.

Time out!

Well-clarified objectives, according to Alan Lakein in *Your Time is Your Life*, need to meet certain specific SMART criteria.

S: specific: so that you know when you have achieved it

M: measurable: by two or more of the following:

     – quantity

     – quality specifications (efficient? effective? other?)

     – cost

A: aligned: with your overall vision and business direction

R: results-focused: is a tangible result expected of me to produce/accomplish?

T: time-based: has a specific due date.

Too often, we confuse tasks with objectives. A task is the action we must take in order to reach the objective. To differentiate between tasks and objectives, we must ask ourselves:

◆ *What* are we trying to achieve *by* completing this task?
◆ What is the benefit of achieving this task?

Example:

Incorrect: to contact five prospects by 31 January 200X.

This is a task, and it does not answer what is the result, or why are we doing this?

Correct: to obtain one client for training services with revenue of . . . by 31 January 200X.

You can see that this is an effective objective because it is:

◆ Specific: one client.
◆ Measurable: size of revenue.
◆ Aligned: one would assume the vision of a consulting firm is to generate revenue!
◆ Results-focused: to obtain the client (result), rather than just contact five prospects (task).
◆ Time-based: by 31 January 200X.

It is critical to define and write down objectives for every aspect of our business within each key result area.

Did you know that. . .

Research conducted at Harvard into graduates 20 years after they had graduated showed the following:

5% were earning more money than the other 95% combined.

The only differentiator was that the 5% had *written down their objectives*. There is something about writing down objectives that affirms our commitment to them, and keeps them 'in sight and in mind'.

The characteristic that gets missed the most is the T: most people state vague terms such as 'within three months'. This is not specific enough – an actual date needs to be set. If the worst happens, and you do not succeed within the time frame, you can simply move the date!

ow are examples of one objective for each key result area for a consulting business. Remember, there may be multiple objectives within each key result area, and we will be showing examples of these different objectives in later chapters.

Key result areas and objectives	
Overall goal:	To operate a thriving consulting business.
Key result area	**Objective(s)**
Finance	To achieve £200,000 in sales with gross margin of 50% in 200X.
Clients	To maintain an active client list of five clients in 200X with no more than 50% income from one client. Client is defined as over £10,000 a year. An active client uses services at least once a quarter.
Business development	To ensure five new clients in 200X with a pipeline of ten prospects and 20 suspects as categorized on the database. Current clients are … Oracle, etc.
Database management	To establish and maintain a database of 500 contacts on ACT, all personally known, by 31 December 200X. To categorize the database by general, suspect and prospect. To maintain contact with the database by distributing three eight-page newsletters and holiday greeting cards.
Product development	To develop and roll out a mini 'call centre assessment' by 1 August 200X.
Operational effectiveness	To maximize operational effectiveness by updating filing system, and implementing new equipment (scanner) by 30 June 200X.
Team development	To establish an ongoing team by December 200X. Team comprises: accountant office manager 2 call centre auditors
Professional development	To become certified in … methodology by attending three *workshops* in 200X.

Exercise 4.3   Writing your objectives

◆ Review the key result areas you identified for your business in Chapter 3. Put these in the key result area form below.

◆ Now write a SMART objective for each key result area below.

Date:_____

My key result areas and objectives	
Overall goal	
Key result area	**Objective(s)**
1.	
2.	
3.	
4.	
5.	
6.	
7.	
8.	
9.	

Are your objectives SMART: specific, measurable, aligned, results-focused, time-based?

◆ Now ask yourself the following questions:
  – Are your objectives definitely outcomes and not tasks?
  – Do they answer the questions: what's the result or what's the benefit?
  – How specific is each objective? How will you know when you've achieved it?
  – How will you measure your objective?
  – Is the objective realistic?
  – Is the objective challenging?
  – Does the objective contain a specific due date?

◆ Make any changes required to make the objectives more SMART.

Coaching point

◆ Some key result areas are easier to measure (e.g. finance) than others (marketing). In these situations, you often have to use the tasks and milestones to provide measurement criteria.
◆ Writing effective objectives is a very complex skill.
◆ There will often be multiple objectives within each key result area.
◆ You may choose to revisit this section when you have completed the more detailed work in the rest of the book on marketing, sales, organizational and financial objectives.

Case study: Joe

Joe has defined some key short-term objectives for himself (short-term objectives are usually less than three months in duration, and can often be part of another larger objective):

Under client management

To achieve one client, for a product launch assessment of no less than £5,000 by 28 February 200X by contacting 20 key prospects.

Under marketing

To decide on an appropriate fee rate by researching five other independent marketing consultants to establish market rates by 1 January 200X.

Within office organization

To ensure a productive office by purchasing a new computer by 31 December, 200X, with ACT and the Microsoft Office Suite.

Establishing milestones

Plans are only good intentions unless they immediately degenerate into hard work.

Peter F. Drucker

When you have established and prioritized your objectives, it is important to decide the key tasks (the things you need to do) and milestones (delivery/completion dates) required to achieve the objectives. Without these tasks and milestones, there is a gap between what you want to do (the objective), and when you are going to do it (the plan). Lack of establishing milestones is the key reason we fail to achieve our objectives. We have to create a list of milestones for **every objective that we have**.

Key result area	Objective
Database management	To establish and maintain a database of 500 contacts on ACT, all personally known, by 31 December 200X. To categorize the database by general, suspect and prospect. To maintain contact with the database by distributing three eight-page newsletters and holiday greeting cards.

Tasks and milestones necessary to complete the objective

Number	What	Who	When	Completed
1	Brainstorm a list of contacts: • friends • family • employers • vendors	SN	30/4/0X	
2	Research database sales tracking system.	DN	14/5/0X	
3	Select sales tracking system.	DN	30/6/0X	
4	Install sales tracking system.	DN	14/7/0X	
5	Input all names on new software.	DN	31/8/0X	
6	Categorize database into general, suspect and prospect.	SN	30/9/0X	

Exercise 4.4   Writing your tasks and milestones

For two of your current key result areas and two objective(s), write down the critical tasks and milestones.

Key result area	Objective(s)			
Number	**What**	**Who**	**When**	**Completed**
1				
2				
3				
4				
5				
6				

Key result area	Objective(s)			
Number	**What**	**Who**	**When**	**Completed**
1				
2				
3				
4				
5				
6				

♦ How will you build up the complete list of tasks associated with each key result area and objective?

_____

_____

♦ What system will you use to track these tasks and milestones?

_____

_____

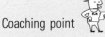

Coaching point

It can be tempting to not write down all these tasks – 'It takes longer to write them down than to do them!' By writing them down, however, we reduce the pressure on our brains and we help to ensure the ideas do not go out of sight and out of mind!

Organizing systems

Consultants vary on the tools they use to track their activities. Some still use a paper-based system such as Filofax or Time Manager. Others use software programs such as Microsoft Project. Others will create a whiteboard and list all the projects and milestones so that they are in sight and in mind. (It's just a little heavy to carry to meetings that's all!)

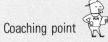

Coaching point

The system you use is not important: the thought process and the organization of the data is key. If the milestones are not written down, first they are easier to forget, and second, you underestimate how many tasks there are at any one time.

Case studies: Marie and Julia

Marie uses her Time Manager system to list her objectives and milestones. Because she worked for this company for five years and is familiar with the system, she believes this is the best way to get started. She has defined her critical milestones and is ready to get out and market her business.

Julia, on the other hand, loves her Palm Pilot to keep her organized. She has put all her phone numbers in the database and is entering her critical action items to track. She enjoys being able to download the contact names and numbers from Outlook and the fact that this can be linked with the Microsoft suite of Office products.

Checklist

1. Have you created your business plan?
2. Have you reviewed the different organization structures and decided which one you will use?
3. Have you consulted with a tax adviser to ensure you understand the implications of this structure?
4. Have you defined objectives for at least three of your key result areas?
5. Have you defined milestones for at least three of these objectives?
6. Have you chosen which system you will use to organize your projects and milestones?

Scorecard

Before leaving this chapter, ask yourself the following questions:

◆ What software or books do you intend to purchase in helping you to write your business plan? How long do you believe your plan needs to be in order to provide you with enough direction, and yet not be too complex? Who else could provide advice in drawing up this plan? Will you use the plan as a tool to help you raise capital?

◆ In terms of your organization structure, what structure will be the most suitable for your needs in the short term? What other resources do you need to support you in this endeavour? How will you ensure you are organized well enough to avoid tax penalties?

◆ When you review your objectives, how clear are they as to the result that they will achieve? Who could look at them and provide you with feedback to ensure they meet the SMART criteria? Are there clear benefits from the goals?

◆ What system will you use to track your milestones and tasks? When will you set up this system? How will you ensure that you keep this system current?

SECTION TWO:
Getting Clients

CHAPTER FIVE

Marketing Your Business

Game plan

One of the greatest challenges that consultants face is getting paying clients. You can demonstrate all the skills in the world, have the best business cards and an articulate business plan, but without clients you have no business! The purpose of this chapter is to help you to:

◆ Begin the process of acquiring clients by creating and implementing a cohesive marketing strategy.

◆ Establish marketing objectives.

◆ Segment the market for your services.

◆ Clearly articulate your range of service offerings and the benefits that they can contribute to the customer.

◆ Decide appropriate promotional strategies.

◆ Build your network.

Creating your marketing plan

> I don't design clothes, I design dreams.
>
> *Ralph Lauren*

Time out!

The *purpose* of your marketing plan is to provide your consulting business with an organized step-by-step approach for raising market awareness. It represents a high-level statement of your business's overall direction, including information on the four P's: *product, promotion, place,* and *price.*

The key elements of your marketing plan are as follows:

Element	Explanation
Market research	Researching potential customers and suppliers to verify that a market for your product exists.
Marketing objectives	Deliverables and outputs that you expect from your marketing activities: how you will know you have succeeded.
Market segmentation	Dividing the market into segments to more easily address customers' needs.
The four 'P's	Product: Defining your product in terms of features and benefits. Promotion: Deciding strategies to raise market awareness. Place: Deciding appropriate distribution channels. Price: Determining fee structures.
Time line/schedule	A tactical outline of actions and milestones.

Foul!

Most people associate marketing with promotional activities. Promotion plays a part in marketing as you can see from the components of the marketing plan above, but there are also many more strategic positioning elements which are necessary to ensure the promotional activities are targeted effectively.

Conducting market research

Researching your audience is vital. A technique that impresses one client with our creativity could be a mere gimmick to another.

Tina Brown, Outside the Box

It is important to conduct market research, not only into the type of consulting you wish to do, but also into the other companies that exist in that marketplace. Market research can be conducted before you leave your current position and provides an ideal way of testing the water. However the extent to which quantitative market research is possible depends on the focus of your consulting business. Much of the consulting market is comprised of individual consultants and therefore it is relatively hard to quantify and document.

Time out!

Objectives for market research are as follows:

◆ To identify whether there is a market for your product or service, and the possible size of your target market.

◆ To assess the existence, size and location of other competitors in your market.

◆ To discover the current pricing structure in your market.

◆ To identify corporate needs.

◆ To evaluate the best way to package your product or service for the market.

◆ To be used as a beginning for the business development process. Many consultants find their first client this way!

Depending on the focus of your business, both formal and informal approaches can be used in the market research process. Formal processes are designed to measure the size and potential market penetration of your service. Informal approaches are designed to obtain a subjective assessment of market potential. Techniques you can use are:

◆ Hire a consultant who specializes in market research to conduct the research for you. You can pay him or her, or organize some type of barter system in exchange for his or her services.

◆ Buy a mailing list for your potential market and distribute a questionnaire to the names on the list about your product or service. Remember the return rate on such a survey is very small – less than 2%. The questionnaire can also be followed up by a phone call, and this will increase the response rate as well as the success of the market assessment.

◆ Create a mailing list of people you know in the industry and send them a questionnaire. You can either ask that the questionnaire be returned, or you can ask to meet directly with them to obtain their feedback.

◆ Call contacts whose opinions you respect, and conduct a short phone interview with them. In this telephone interview, you could ask such questions as: 'If you were in my shoes, what would you do?' 'Who do you think would be interested in the services?' 'What else might they be interested in?'

◆ Research trade associations in your field and either attend meetings for networking reasons or use their list of members to target for research.

◆ Attend cocktail parties and other social functions to network.

◆ Use the Internet and conduct a search looking for companies providing similar services.

◆ Use the want ads in the newspaper and industry magazines: these are a great source of information about small companies.

◆ Read current trade publications.

◆ A combination of the above.

Case study: Marie

Marie has spent some time in marketing in a previous job, and so has already completed much of her marketing planning. Because her industry is highly dispersed, she has decided to conduct informal market research by talking to people she knows who are both consultants and possible clients. She has created a list of 30 people, who she plans to talk to in the next three weeks. Her main purpose in these calls is to determine market interest for her product and service, and to understand current market rates.

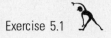 Exercise 5.1　Deciding your market research approach

Thinking about the type of consulting you wish to undertake and the market for your services, answer the following questions:

- How easy is it for you to measure the market for your service quantitatively?

- How much research do you think you could undertake on the Internet?

- How many people do you know who might be able to provide you with insight into the market?

- What upcoming events do you know of that you could attend/participate in, in order to find out more about the market for your service?

- Based on these questions, list below three specific market research activities you will undertake with specific deadlines.

Tasks and milestones necessary to conduct market research:

Number	What	Who	When	Completed
1				
2				
3				

Coaching point

While conducting market research could appear to be 'avoiding asking for business', the increased knowledge and confidence that it can provide to you will be invaluable in getting your business started on a sound footing.

Establishing marketing objectives

Based on your unique selling proposition and your vision, you need to create marketing objectives for your business. More detail on the criteria for effective objectives are included in Chapter 4. Remember these objectives need to meet the SMART criteria outlined earlier. They need to be:

S – specific
M – measurable
A – aligned
R – results-focused
T – time-based

There is normally a variety of marketing goals for a consulting business under several categories:

◆ share of the market
◆ market penetration
◆ market visibility
◆ target market
◆ promotional activities
◆ pricing
◆ size of database
◆ number of newsletters.

Make sure you set specific objectives for your marketing plan – what is not measured does not get done! If you don't reach that objective, it is easier to change it than to have not created it at all.

Case study: Julia

Julia has defined two short-term objectives for her marketing activities:

◆ To raise market visibility with start-up organizations by distributing via e-mail a human resources newsletter providing tips and techniques on common small company issues to over 100 organizations (from a mailing list she purchased), to generate a minimum of two follow-up enquiries by 31 August 200X.

◆ To create two strategic partnerships with venture capital firms in order to obtain at least one referral by 30 September 200X.

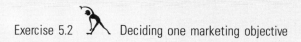

Exercise 5.2   Deciding one marketing objective

Thinking about the type of consulting you wish to undertake and the market for your services, define one specific marketing objective for your business below:

Marketing key result areas	Objective(s)
Is it SMART?	

◆ Make sure the objective has a specific deadline and you are clear about the outcome you are expecting.

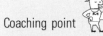

Coaching point

As you continue to work through this marketing chapter, make sure you set objectives for other key activities.

Segmenting the market

Segmenting the market involves breaking down the market into smaller sub-sections. The benefit of segmenting the market is that you can then target marketing efforts more effectively. The segmentation can be made by:

◆ industry, such as retail, software, hardware, wholesale, telecommunications, non-profit
◆ geographical area, such as England, UK, Europe, USA
◆ company size such as small (under 100 people), medium, large
◆ maturity of company: start-up, mature
◆ type of company culture
◆ functional category such as human resources, web page design, training, marketing

◆ functional speciality within functional category: e.g. within human resources there are the functional specialities of payroll, compensation, benefits and recruiting.

Case study: Joe

Joe decided that he wanted to offer project management services in launching new products to mid-sized high-tech companies along the M4 corridor.

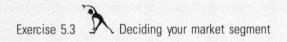

Exercise 5.3   Deciding your market segment

Thinking about the type of consulting you wish to undertake and the market for your services, answer the questions below to help you segment your market:

◆ To what extent do you wish to travel? Is there a natural geographic focus to the type of consulting you will be undertaking?

◆ What specific market expertise do you possess, e.g. retail, software, etc? Is there a specific market segment that you wish to focus on?

◆ What specific functional expertise do you possess? (e.g. product marketing, finance, HR, etc).

◆ Is there a specific size of company that would benefit from your services?

◆ In what market segment (whether as an employee or a consultant) have you had your greatest success?

◆ Now list your ideas for market segments you want to focus on below:

_____

_____

_____

_____

Coaching point

Don't be worried that by trying to segment the market you might miss opportunities. These segments are guidelines only. Initially there is a tendency to take any work that is offered! As your business matures, it is often more beneficial and less risky to segment your market in more detail.

Defining your product or service: the first 'P'

A sweet, brown, fizzy beverage…Coca Cola is one of the world's truly non-essential products brilliantly marketed.

Wall Street Journal

This stage in the marketing process involves defining the services you offer in terms of:

◆ Features: The features of a product or service include facts, function information, its characteristics, its design or its construction. Customers usually buy features only when they relate to benefits.

◆ Benefits: A benefit is anything that contributes to an improvement in condition, produces an advantage, or aids in accomplishing a task. It is the *positive result* or *bonus* achieved as a result of using your product or service. It shows how a company will gain from using these services as well as what the services can do. It answers the questions 'What's in it for me?' or 'What's in it for the company?'

It is important to define your product or service in user-friendly terms through the use of features and benefits, specifically in relation to how they meet business needs. Customers are interested in benefits, but we are often most comfortable talking about features.

Time out!
A benefit answers the questions:
◆ Who cares?
◆ So what?
A transition statement to link the feature to the benefit is:
◆ Which means that . . .

Benefits can also be **tangible** (the benefit can be measured objectively) or they can be **intangible**. Benefits combined create the **ultimate benefit**: this represents the overall benefit of the product or service to the user.

Features and benefits of a table

Below are examples of the features and benefits of a table: a tangible product to illustrate how this process works.

Feature	Which means that Who cares? So what?	Benefit	Ultimate benefit
Four legs	Which means that	The table is stable (tangible)	} Efficient working space
Brown	Which means that	The table is aesthetically pleasing (intangible)	
14-square feet of surface area	Which means that	It is spacious and holds a lot of material (tangible)	

Features and benefits of services

It is harder to think about a service in terms of features and benefits because a service itself is intangible, and varies from one moment to another and according to the customer's mood at any one time.

> Time out!
>
> Describing a service such as consulting differs considerably from describing a product like an automobile. A car is manufactured in one location and then delivered for sale to the customer in another. A service is often created and delivered simultaneously. As a result of conducting a consulting project, you concurrently deliver it. Goods are produced, services are performed. These differences pose a special challenge to consultants.

How do you make relatively invisible services seem real and useful to prospective clients? This is achieved by making sure the services are understood, and by somehow making them more tangible, using features and benefits.

It is also harder to think about a service without a specific customer in mind because most services will be designed and delivered to meet a specific customer need. However the mental exercise of differentiating between your consulting service's features and benefits will help you in the sales interaction and as you are creating marketing collateral for yourself (as described later in this chapter).

Features and benefits: consulting and making money at it

Let's look at one example of features and benefits for a service: an eight-hour training programme on *Consulting and Making Money At It*.

Feature	Which means that Who cares? So what?	Benefit	Ultimate benefit
One day programme	Which means that	Time effective (tangible)	
Learn marketing strategies	Which means that	Increase exposure (intangible) and get clients (tangible)	**Successful consulting business**
Participant materials are supplied as a reference tool	Which means that	Greater retention (intangible)	
Interactive with exercises and discussion	Which means that	Greater learning (tangible)	

Case study: Frank

Frank offers a range of services, but he is particularly focusing on the Support Centre Review of Operational Processes he performs. As you can see from the list below, this one service provides comprehensive tangible and intangible benefits to a potential customer and can be linked easily to business results. Customer satisfaction normally links to greater loyalty and customer retention.

Frank's services: review of operational effectiveness

Feature	Which means that Who cares? So what?	Benefit	Ultimate benefit
Call flow and handling analysis	Which means that	Improve productivity in call flow	Higher customer satisfaction
Problem handling and resolution	Which means that	Quicker problem resolution time	
Internal and external customer service level agreements	Which means that	Increased efficiency	
Complete process flow analysis	Which means that	Improved process flow	
Complete measurement and reporting	Which means that	Enables continuous improvement and proactive service	
People: staff skill analysis and recommendations	Which means that	Greater employee retention	
Tools and technologies assessment and improvement recommendations	Which means that	Reduced cost of solving problems Increased contribution margin	

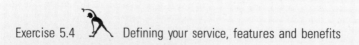

Exercise 5.4   Defining your service, features and benefits

Thinking about the type of consulting you wish to undertake and the market for your services, answer the questions below to help you define your service offerings:

- What are the key services you have been planning to offer to your clients?
- What are the specific components of these service offerings (see Frank's case study for more examples)?
- What business results could these services contribute to?

◆ How did you measure success when you were offering these services within an organization?
◆ Now try to complete the table below.

Features and benefits: your services

Feature	Which means that Who cares? So what?'	Benefit	Ultimate benefit
	Which means that		
	Which means that		
	Which means that		
	Which means that		

Coaching point

Writing features and benefits is not easy for several reasons.

1. As you are getting started, you may not be clear about the specific services that you are offering. Still, if you are not clear, probably the customer isn't either!

2. Often it is easier to define features and benefits when we have a specific customer in mind – this can help to crystallize how they will benefit from the services.

3. The process of differentiating between features and benefits itself is not easy.

Despite these challenges, try to do your best with the exercise: it will help you clarify your thought processes and it will prevent you from having your first piece of marketing material focus only on features!

Foul!

One of the biggest mistakes you can make as a consultant is to deluge the client in information about your service features without mentioning their benefits. If you talk about features for too long, you will be able to see their facial expression show 'Who cares? So what?', but they are probably too polite to say this out loud! Sometimes you need to talk only about benefits.

Deciding your promotional plan: the second 'P'

You are every bit as much of a brand as Nike, Coke, Pepsi and The Body Shop.

Tom Peters

Once you have identified your potential clients and clarified your marketing plan, you need to determine the most appropriate promotional strategies for building your brand and acquiring clients. All too often, consultants randomly select marketing tools. They might hand out brochures, give speeches and make personal calls. However these consultants often can't explain why they selected these tools over others. They have not targeted their clients nor defined their message adequately.

Time out!
Your promotional plan should include some or all of the following:
◆   advertising
◆   public relations
◆   marketing communications
◆   giving speeches
◆   trade shows and exhibitions
◆   web page
◆   newsletters and mailings.

The purpose of the promotional strategies is to create leads for, and awareness of, your consulting business. As you can see in the funnel shown in Chapter 6, promotional activity helps to raise awareness and create interest, but does not confirm a need. *Only when your business is established will promotional activities directly produce revenue.* Remember not to use undertaking promotional strategies as an excuse for not calling or meeting with clients!

Promotion is necessary therefore to:

◆   begin the process of obtaining new clients
◆   raise interest in your product or service
◆   increase awareness of your business
◆   establish or modify your image

- educate the public through your efforts
- attract new employees
- provide a public service.

Once you identify your potential clients and clarify your marketing plan, you need to determine the most appropriate promotional strategies for raising awareness and interest from potential clients. Let's review ideas and strategies within each of the key categories.

Fig. 5.1 Promotional activities.

Advertising

Advertising is used to raise awareness and promote interest in a product or service. Advertising results are hard to quantify, and the advertising needs to be repeated at set intervals to obtain any benefits. When starting your consulting business, if advertising is used at all, it needs to be extremely selective and focused on the particular market or industry segment where your consulting provides value. Depending on your functional expertise, you may want to consider the following possibilities:

- *Yellow Pages*
- local newspapers
- trade directory
- conference publications
- exhibition catalogues
- local association newsletters
- web search engines such as Google and Yahoo!

Advertising

Advantages	*Disadvantages*
◆ begins to build a market awareness	◆ can be expensive
◆ can often stimulate interest	◆ for a service, is unlikely to create a need to buy

Foul!

Remember, one advertisement in a publication is not going to succeed in raising awareness. Instead consider placing multiple advertisements (for instance in a trade journal every month for three months) or in a publication that has a long shelf life so that it may be referred to on more than one occasion.

Public relations

Public relations are often viewed as unpaid advertising: it means that your business gains exposure in trade publications without a monetary payment from you, and as a result carries more credibility.

Time out!

Public relations includes publishing articles and books, submitting articles, being quoted in the business press, undertaking a formal public relations campaign such as issuing press releases, targeting specific journalists, and obtaining local radio or TV exposure.

Published articles and books can establish and enhance both your image and your reputation, particularly if you have a specific story to tell within your area of expertise. There are more than 7,000 trade publications in the USA, most of which actively seek material. Again you should write for journals whose readers can use your services. Be aware however that writing is very time-consuming and it is hard to guarantee or quantify results.

PR

Advantages	*Disadvantages*
◆ 'unpaid advertising'	◆ writing is very time-consuming
◆ more credibility than 'paid advertising'	◆ no guaranteed results
◆ greater market awareness.	◆ great strategy to avoid talking to 'real people'

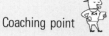

Coaching point

If you choose to undertake a PR campaign, you may consider using a specialist PR agency to support you. If you do, make sure you research their background and success, and be realistic about what you expect them to achieve. So much of PR involves being in the right place at the right time.

Marketing communications

Marketing communications encompasses brochures, business cards and cover letters.

Brochures

With the availability of desktop publishing, it has become easier to avoid the high costs of producing brochures. In the early stages of consulting, a professionally produced summary of qualifications in the form of a c.v. is adequate. Clients expect brochures but most often as a back-up device.

Foul!

Remember, people buy people – *not* paper! Make sure you don't spend time creating a brochure as an excuse for not talking to potential clients.

Coaching point

Make sure your brochure lists *benefits* as well as *features*.

Initially you can use simple data sheets including:

◆ introductory text
◆ overview of service
◆ business results expected
◆ objectives
◆ biography.

Business cards

Business cards are an essential part of building your business's corporate identity. However they are a tool best used face-to-face, so do not use creating a business card as an excuse for not talking to prospective customers. Use of business cards varies from culture to culture, so make sure you familiarize yourself with local customs when you are travelling to a new country.

Coaching point

There are resources on the web that provide a limited number of free business cards in exchange for advertising their services on the back of the card: see the appendix for more information. Consider including the following on your business card: your name, address, phone number, mobile number, fax number, e-mail address, web site (if you have one), and if possible some type of visual logo and statement that reflects your business.

Cover letters

Cover letters support your brochure and/or proposal when marketing your services. They need to be personally written for each client, addressing specific issues regarding that client's needs and the way you can meet those needs. (Proposals will be discussed in detail in the next chapter.)

Marketing communications

Advantages	Disadvantages
◆ necessary for client contact	◆ difficult to create providing a 'one size fits all' description of services
◆ an important tool in creating and communicating your image	◆ time-consuming to create

Giving free speeches

Speeches are frequently used to familiarize clients with consultants' capabilities. Of course your topic must be timely and your presentation professional.

Free speeches

Advantages	Disadvantages
◆ gives you credibility within a specific subject area ◆ allows you to personally demonstrate your verbal capability	◆ time-consuming – remember, for one hour's presentation, it takes eight hours of preparation ◆ free speeches may generate many more free speeches! ◆ giving free speeches places your product in the 'free' category.

Coaching point

If you decide to conduct free speeches, make sure you research these opportunities to ensure your target audience will be attending. There's nothing worse then presenting the right content to the wrong people!

In addition, be clear about the outcome you are expecting from the speech. Do you want to generate leads or is this speech a way of establishing credibility within a specific field? Either is possible, but being clear about results can reduce disappointments.

Foul!

Often consultants think they would like to do keynote speeches – very little time and lots of money! However, providing these types of speeches is very competitive (normally requiring a successful book) and you may have to invest in developing professional video tapes of previous speeches to supply to prospective clients. Not quite the easy money that it looks!

Trade shows and exhibitions

In the early stages of your business, trade shows can appear to be an expensive investment. However it is always possible to attend trade shows:

◆ as a delegate in a professional development activity
◆ to build a network
◆ to conduct market research
◆ to identify possible strategic alliances

- to raise awareness by advertising in trade show guides
- to get information on competition.

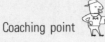
Coaching point

Attending trade shows can be a very cost-effective way of killing several birds with one stone!

Web pages

As Internet use continues to grow, web-based marketing activities will become more critical to new business development. According to Microsoft, approximately 60% of the small businesses that have access to email currently have their own web site. Some organizations have eliminated conventional marketing channels to replace them with web-based sales and distribution. Other organizations use web-based marketing to supplement their marketing efforts.

According to research conducted by Booz Allen in 2004 for the Department of Trade and Industry . . .

- The proportion of micro and small businesses with a web site increased by 16 percentage points in 2004 from 2003.
- 73% of businesses provide information about products and services for customers on line.

Web sites

Advantages	Disadvantages
◆ inexpensive promotional channel	◆ no personal recommendation – you will have to meet with any prospective organization
◆ a wide range of audiences have access to it	
◆ geographic boundaries are eliminated	◆ the web has millions of sites so your product/service could get lost
◆ easy and quick to put together and change	◆ many unqualified leads could get time-consuming
◆ requires minimal technical expertise	
◆ a way of quickly and easily providing information to people who inquire	◆ it is better used as a support to existing customers and prospects than to generate business

Coaching point

◆ Wait to set up your web site until you are somewhat clear on the products and services you will be offering – if you are not clear, the web site certainly will not be either!

◆ Setting up a web site does not require an extensive capital outlay – there are many independent consultants out there who can help to create a site.

◆ Try to make sure the web site is updated at least once a year to keep it fresh and current.

◆ Spend some time 'surfing the web' and make notes on what you like about sites and what annoys you.

Newsletters and mailings

If you have unique information to share, or wish to keep in contact with those on your database when you are busy, newsletters are an effective communication tool. In addition, if you index your database you can then mail articles you read on specific topics to specific people. For instance, if some of your customers are interested in customer service, you could mail them an interesting customer service article you have read with a brief note attached to it.

Newsletters and mailings

Advantages	Disadvantages
◆ cost-effective way of keeping contact with your database	◆ they take time to create
◆ excellent 'soft' sales tool – reminds customers of you without asking for anything	◆ there is no 'real reason' to do, therefore this activity often drops off the bottom of the 'radar'
◆ great way of keeping the database current – you will know if people have moved because mailshots are returned	

Coaching point

Newsletters and mailing can include such items as Christmas cards, articles, sending current business updates and upcoming events. Increasingly these newsletters are being sent electronically, resulting in cost savings and speedier access. Remember the disadvantage of this medium – many people do not download attachments and if the update is in the email, it's hard to make the content look attractive.

Case study: Joe initiates his promotional activities

Using the web, Joe has conducted market research into other consultants who provide services, and into the market size. Based on the projected growth of his market and the increasing pressure to reduce time to market, he believes his business will be viable. He uses email to initiate contacts with the people he finds on the web and is planning to establish strategic partnerships with local marketing companies as an additional resource if they are overloaded or do not have his specific expertise. He has created his own web page to demonstrate his capabilities. Joe has linked his web page to other product marketing web sites to facilitate prospects 'finding him'. He is investigating costs for advertising in local and national magazines, although he thinks that this could prove to be too expensive. He is going to attend a product marketing conference and is considering placing an advertisement in the conference publication. In addition, he has bought an email distribution list and he plans to email an attachment describing his services. Joe has created an email list of friends and colleagues and plans to send them the attachment describing his services.

Exercise 5.5 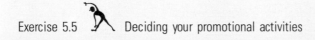 Deciding your promotional activities

Thinking about the type of consulting you wish to undertake and the market for your services, answer the questions opposite to help you prioritize your promotional activities.

Coaching point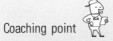

It can be tempting to undertake lots of promotional activities in quick succession. Bear in mind that many of these techniques are time-consuming, so in order to be able to evaluate the success of each, you may want to introduce each in a more structured way.

Promotional activities	Questions	Actions
Advertising	What specific trade publications do you read? Refer to? How long is the 'shelf life' of each advertisement? What figures can the publications provide on their readership? Response rates?	
Press relations	What journalists do you know? What contacts might you be able to leverage in the press? What is a unique story that you could tell? What subject material would help you in establishing your credibility?	
Marketing communications	What is the minimum written documentation you require? What resources could you use to help you in graphic layout? What is the key message that you wish to include on all documents?	
Free speeches	What target audiences would it be worth presenting to? What would you want to achieve from giving speeches? Is there another way you could achieve the same goal? What would be a worthwhile subject to present?	
Trade shows and exhibitions	What are the major exhibitions for your market segment? What speakers are presenting at each? What are the themes? What would you want to achieve from each show? What planning can you do to ensure you capitalize on the time there?	
Web site	What is the key information that you would like to include on your web site? Who do you know who could help you create your web site? Are there any other ways you can use your web site: questionnaires, quizzes, interactive exercises, checklists, etc which would increase the functionality of your web site? What do you want to achieve from establishing a web site?	
Newsletters and mailings	What types of news, information, and articles could you communicate to your database? What would be the best medium for your newsletter – paper? Electronic? Both? How can you increase the possibility of a response? (Reply button on email; tear off slip in hard copy, etc) How can you gather other information to distribute to your database?	

Selecting distribution channels: the third 'P'

As a consultant there are more limited distribution channels: building your network, performing sub-contract work and establishing strategic partnerships.

> The key to any personal branding is word-of-mouth marketing...so the big trick to building your brand is to find ways to nurture your network of colleagues.
>
> *Tom Peters*

Your network is your prime distribution strategy. Referrals by past or present clients are the most commonly used means of obtaining new business. A survey made by the Institute of Management Consultants suggests that repeat business constitutes 70% of all business while referrals make up 15%. Networking is very important for marketing yourself, particularly in the early stages. Here are a few guidelines for establishing and formalizing your network:

◆ build the network
◆ consolidate the network onto a database.

Build the network

> Time out!
> Your network should number between 200 and 400 people. It will be a dynamic, constantly changing promotional tool that you can expect to turn over approximately 25% (and up to 50%) per annum.

Although this sounds like a large number of people, you create a network by identifying all the people you know (your primary contacts) as well as your secondary contacts (those people you have been referred to).

Your network comes from:

◆ friends
◆ family

- colleagues, past and present
- university, alumni associations
- trade organizations
- neighbours
- the pub
- sports clubs
- people you meet when travelling
- prospects from presentations
- contacts from exhibitions and conferences
- vendors/suppliers from previous jobs.

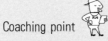

Coaching point

The best criteria to consider are:

- you personally know the person
- you respect the person
- the people on the list would probably like to hear from you
- you ensure that there is a mutual exchange of benefits/information
- the person on your network would remember you i.e. that you probably have met them more than once.

Foul!

Make sure you are not acting like the 'networking barracuda' who appears to always have something to sell and whom people avoid like the plague!

It is impossible to talk to 200 people often, so you might want to use one or more of the following to stay in touch:

- newsletter
- email
- Christmas card/letter.

the network onto an electronic database

: ideally should have an individual's name, company name, job title, phone number, fax number, email address, and some sort of contact information. It is better to record your network on some type of database/sales management tool such as ACT, Outlook, etc, not on a Rolodex or business cards because:

- this provides easy access for mailing and newsletters
- it is centrally available
- it is convenient to update
- it is possible to sort the database by category.

Time out!

Try classifying your network into the following categories:

General contacts: the world at large.

Suspects: suspects are pre-qualified in some way. They probably won't give you business, but know someone who might. They are influencers and should compose about 25% of your network.

Prospects: these are people with a current defined need.

Clients: these are people for whom you have done work during the past year. There should be about ten to 20 names on this list.

Key clients: the two to five people you are currently doing work for. This makes up the largest part of your current revenue.

Interest in a specific area: you may also want to sort your database by your contact's prospective interests in your service, for instance teams and consulting.

In the next chapter we will review how this database can be used proactively in your business development process.

Case study: Marie

One of Marie's marketing goals is to establish a database of over 200 names on Outlook. She has already established over 100 names on her database through internal clients she worked with as Director of Training, a few people from the training association she is a member of, vendors who supplied her when she was Director of Training, contacts from her previous consulting experience, other trainers and friends who are active working professionals.

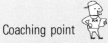

Exercise 5.6   Building your network

Think about people you would like to include in your network:

♦ Whose opinion do you respect?

♦ Who do you think would have good ideas for you?

♦ Look at the different categories outlined earlier: friends, family, etc. List all the people you would like to maintain contact with in each group.

♦ Who are 'influencers/thought leaders' in their field?

♦ Look at your Christmas card list – who should be in your database also?

Take a break and then return to the list and see if you can add more names.

What automated system will you use to track your database and why?

_____

_____

_____

Coaching point

◆ Most people initially believe that they do not know enough people to populate a database and yet when they take the time to stop and think about the people they know, they have no trouble building the database to at least 200 people.

Pricing your product: the fourth 'P'

This will be discussed in detail in Chapter 7.

Creating a marketing schedule

As a consultant, it is important to plan your marketing strategy. Often time taken in this area directly detracts from time spent in the most critical part of the consulting process: actually talking to and influencing clients. There are many prospective consultants who have great brochures and no customers!

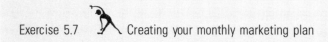

Exercise 5.7   Creating your monthly marketing plan

◆ When you integrate all the marketing activities onto one plan, make sure you are realistic about time commitments in each area.

Marketing	Week one	Week two	Week three	Week four
Market research				
Setting market objectives				
Deciding market segments				
Defining your product				
Deciding promotional activities				
Building your network				

Coaching point

If you know who, why, what and how you plan to market, then you must only decide when.

Your timing should consider three factors:

◆ When the client is most receptive.

◆ When the client is least likely to receive competitors' messages.

◆ When your resources will permit you to both market and to meet the demand created by marketing.

Checklist

Have you:

1. Conducted initial market research into your area of expertise?
2. Established three clear marketing goals?
3. Defined clearly the business needs your product and service address?
4. Identified three competitors and defined how you differ from them?
5. Analysed market segments and defined three markets for your business service?
6. Prioritized your promotional activity and established a promotional plan for the next three months?
7. Created a list of 200 people?
8. Bought a database program to track your database activities?

 Scorecard

Before leaving this chapter, ask yourself the following questions:

◆ In terms of your marketing plan, what do you consider to be the market for your product or service? How comfortable are you establishing marketing goals and what segments do you wish to concentrate on initially?

◆ What promotional strategies are best for your business? What are the personal challenges you face in defining and deciding to use these strategies? What time commitment will you allocate to your promotional efforts?

◆ What size network will you need to be able to facilitate your business growth? What are your personal reservations about contacting people you know for advice and how will you address these concerns? How will you categorize your database and ensure you are focusing on those people who will help to grow your business, not just those you like?

CHAPTER SIX

Selling your Service

 Game plan

The most challenging part of consulting is finding clients! Marketing looks at the big picture of informing the public of your services. Selling is a specific marketing activity that results in a consulting assignment. The difference between successful and unsuccessful consultants is usually their ability to sell.

The purpose of this chapter is to help you to:

- Overcome your resistance to selling.
- Understand the sales process to maximize activity at each stage.
- Establish sales objectives to guide your activity.
- Improve your sales effectiveness using email, on the telephone and face-to-face.
- Structure your assignments using proposals and contracts to ensure client satisfaction.

Overcoming your fear of selling

Nothing happens until someone sells something.

Source Unknown

 Foul!

When we hear the word SELL, often the first thing that comes to mind is:

- used car salesmen!
- pushy tactics!

- telephone marketing calls in the evening over dinner!
- unsolicited products or services.

Time out!

SELL = HELP

Instead of thinking about *selling* to your customers, change two letters S and L and think about *helping* them instead. When you provide a service to clients, you will be helping them meet a business need, solve a problem or achieve a business goal. If you cannot help them, then don't sell to them!

Selling at its best is a mutually satisfying interaction in which both sides win. On the one hand, the client's needs are met. On the other hand, the consultant generates income, engages in his or her profession, and reaps personal rewards for helping the client. In addition, selling ourselves can be simpler than selling a product – we know what we can do. But it can also be more difficult because a refusal can be viewed as a personal rejection.

Exercise 6.1 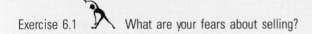 What are your fears about selling?

Thinking about your consulting business, answer the following questions:

- How do you feel about the need to sell?

- What are your biggest challenges you face in selling to clients?

- How could you overcome these challenges?

- What are your biggest strengths in selling to clients?

- How could you capitalize on these strengths?

Coaching point

To overcome a fear of selling, follow three steps:

1. Realize why selling is in your best interest.
2. Understand the emotional response behind your fears.
3. Learn the skills that enable you to sell successfully.

Case study: Marie

Marie learnt when she was working at the training company that selling, for the most part, did not involve the 'dreaded cold calling'! Instead, she knew that if she maintained her database of contacts and used a gentler networking approach, over time she would have as much business as she needed.

Understanding the sales process

In the modern world of business, it is useless to be a creative original thinker unless you can also sell what you create. Management cannot be expected to recognize a good idea unless it is presented to them by a good salesman.

David M. Ogilvy

In order to be able to sell successfully, it is important to understand the stages in the sales process as listed below:

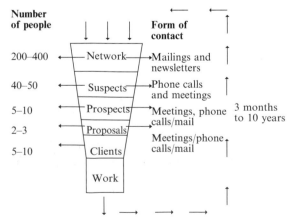

Fig. 6.1 The sales process. The steps in this process are outlined on the next page.

Category	Definition	Maintaining contac
Your network	As we discussed in Chapter 5, your network is the key building block for your business. From this base of 200–400 people, you will probably generate 95% of your new business opportunities. However if you tried to contact this network personally, you would become submerged in email, returning phone calls and meeting people, and would be unable to focus on the key individuals who can help you grow your business.	To ensure your database is kept current and you don't lose touch with people, the following can be used: • newsletter • mailing • cards • bulk emails.
Suspects	These individuals do not have a defined need as yet, but they are the contacts from whom future business is likely to arise. Suspects normally number about 20–25% or your database of approximately 40–50 people. Suspects can fit into the following categories: • they are pre-qualified in some way • they may be influencers in the industry • they may be other consultants who you might use for work and might also require your services • they are decision-makers in their area • they are brokers in the industry you are in • they are leading edge thinkers • they possess some type of unique content knowledge.	With suspects you wish to develop the relationship in a more personal way using: • phone • personal emails • limited face-to-face meetings.
Prospects	Prospective leads have the ability to buy, the right to buy and the need to buy, often within a short time period. Your sales funnel at any one time will have between five and ten prospects depending on the size and maturity of your business. Your prospects come from two sources: your marketing efforts and your personal contact system (suspects and network).	As people tend to buy people, most of the interaction with prospects is conducted in: • phone calls • face-to-face meetings, There may be two to three meetings as the prospect's needs are refined and the sales process continues.
Proposals	Proposals are normally the final part of the sales process where you document the information and approach you have discussed with the prospect. At any one time, you will probably have two to three proposals outstanding.	Proposals are sent by: • email • fax • hard copy.
Clients	If you are successful in clearly defining the client requirements, often the prospect will become a client. At any one time, a consulting business probably needs between five to ten clients. If the business only has one client, then it may be exposed if there is a sudden change in client's strategy.	Regular contact is inherent in conducting the project.

Case study: Frank's funnel in action

Frank has established and prioritized his database, and has sent a general email flyer to his entire network providing a brief overview of his new venture and contact information. He identified ten key decision-makers for his suspect list. He believes that for his sort of services, long-term contract work, he needed only two to three prospects at any point in time. He was concerned that because each assignment could last several months, if he overloaded his sales funnel he might not be able to cope with the demand. He sent each of these people an email note outlining what he was planning to do, and then followed up a week later with phone calls. From these ten contacts, he was able to talk to five people, after two or three call-backs, which resulted in a meeting with a server company. This lead came from the current Vice-President who used to be his boss at a previous organization. He is planning to meet them next week, and while they seemed to want only a short-term needs assessment project, he feels fairly confident that he will be able to take on this short-term project and build more work from it. In addition he has called several people with whom he used to work directly. He has also scheduled two meetings with other consultants in the industry, to start to build a collaborative network and to find out more about how they market and sell their services.

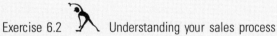

Exercise 6.2   Understanding your sales process

Thinking about your consulting business, draw a funnel and then fill in your funnel using the table opposite.

Coaching point
◆ If this process is working effectively the time taken to close business, i.e. move down the funnel, may be as little as three months. It could also take years!
◆ If you talk to someone just as they identify a need it could be even quicker. And today the sales cycle is definitely shortening as the rate of change in the world increases.
◆ However, there is normally a time delay between when you originally make contact and when you begin to find solid prospects.
◆ Don't get discouraged if you are making all the right efforts but haven't found a client yet. That is all part of the mystery that is sales!

Category	Questions to answer	Maintaining contact
Your network	How large a network do you think you have? How large a network do you think you need? How could you build this network further?	How will you initially contact your network? What will you say? How often do you plan to contact them in your first year?
Suspects	How many suspects do you need for your type of business? How could you build your list of suspects?	How will you contact your list of suspects?
Prospects	How many prospects do you need for your type of business? How could you build your list of prospects?	How will you contact your prospects?
Proposals	How many proposals do you need for your type of business? How could you cover a project if you became overloaded?	How will you follow up and track your proposals?
Clients	How many clients do you need for your type of business? How could you ensure you generate more business from existing clients?	How will you maintain contact with your clients?

Time out!

Remember:

◆ It can take five calls and numerous emails to secure a meeting.

◆ It can take two to three meetings before you submit a proposal.

◆ It can take days/weeks and months for clients to make a decision.

◆ Even if they decide to use you and you do the work, it could be 60 days after that before you receive any income!

Establishing sales objectives

Flaming enthusiasm, backed up by horse sense and persistence, is the quality that most frequently makes for success.

Dale Carnegie

Without a selling orientation you can easily overlook activities necessary for the continuation of your consulting practice. By establishing realistic yet challenging objectives for each part of the sales process, you can prevent the nightmare of running out of consulting projects and avoid the 'feast or famine' syndrome.

Remember! These goals need to meet 'SMART' criteria as outlined in Chapter 4.

S   – specific

M   – measurable

A   – aligned

R   – results-focused

T   – time-based.

Exercise 6.3 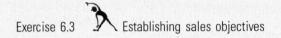 Establishing sales objectives

Thinking about your consulting business, create objectives using the table below:

Category	Objectives and things to consider
Your network	Size of network and frequency of contact.
Suspects	Number of suspects and targets for frequency of contact.
Prospects	Number of prospects and targets for frequency of contact.
Proposals	Number of proposals per month.
Clients	Number of clients per year, average reorder value, number of new clients per year.
Other	Number of meetings per week.

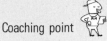
Coaching point
The more specific you are the greater are the chances of success.

Evaluating sales communication channels

Establishing positive sales communication with your clients represents a complex combination of means and method.

- Means includes evaluating and using communication channels effectively.
- Method includes understanding differences and applying a range of simple and complex interpersonal skills to adapt to differing client needs.

Let's look at communication channels first.

Time out!
There are numerous communication channels available to use through which to interact with clients including:
- email
- voicemail
- telephone
- informal coffee/lunch meetings
- formal meetings
- presentations.

Increasingly, more and more of our communication takes place via email. While email is a great communication channel, it is always important to use the right medium for the message.

Foul!
Remember the concept of a 'quick email' is an oxymoron!

Most emails will take approximately five minutes to write, spell-check and send. And for anyone who disputes this fact, think about the number of emails you receive, which have obviously only taken one minute to write, that you have no idea what the person is talking about!

Take a look at the list below:

Email is great for...
◆ Multiple distribution of the same information
◆ Giving instructions
interaction
◆ Creating a paper trail in commitments
◆ Communicating specific facts and data
◆ Summarizing follow-up commitments
◆ Communicating with lots of people at the same time
◆ Confirming a buying decision

Email is not so good for...
◆ Initiating relationships
◆ Communicating about feelings
◆ An issue that needs real-time

◆ Urgent issues
◆ Obtaining a buying decision

Real time interaction is great for...
◆ Initiating relationships
◆ Communicating about feelings
◆ Building trust
◆ Identifying needs
◆ Presenting solutions
◆ Dealing with issues that need person-to-person interaction
◆ Urgent issues
◆ Closing a sale

Real time interaction is not so good for...
◆ Dissemination of facts and data (with no discussion)
◆ Giving instructions
◆ Tracking specific facts and data

Exercise 6.4 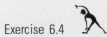 Which communication channel do you prefer to use?

Thinking about the way you tend to interact with clients and others, answer the following questions:

◆ How much of your communication is via email?

- How do you feel about using the phone?
- How much of your interaction is face to face?
- To what extent are you using your real-time interaction (phone and meetings) on suspects, prospects and clients?
- How can you make sure you are using the right medium for the message?

_____

_____

_____

_____

Case study: Joe

Joe really enjoys person-to-person interaction. In fact, he would prefer to be talking to someone than working alone, writing or planning. When Joe analysed his use of communication channels using the exercise above, he discovered that he was spending too much time interacting with his network, which although fun, was not allowing him sufficient time for planning and research. He started to use email a little more, sending interesting articles and information to his network, and concentrated his face-to-face time on new suspects and potential prospects with whom he wanted to build rapport.

Preparing your 30-second commercial

It is important, whether you will be meeting people in person or on the phone, to prepare your 30-second commercial so that when someone asks you, 'What do you do?' you don't say 'Well, duh, I am just getting started, and uh...!'

A simple model for preparing your 30-second commercial is to briefly review four specific sections. Any longer than that time and people will not listen.

Time out!

In your commercial include:

1. Your personal background and/or your connection to the person.
2. Your educational background, particularly if this will enhance your credibility.

3.   Your business background: a few summary statements providing your key areas of expertise and unique selling proposition.
4.   The bridge connecting what you are doing as a consultant and what help or advice you are looking for from them.

Case study: Marie

Personal: Hi. My name is . . . and we met at the . . . meeting last week where you asked me to follow up with you this week.

Educational background: I have a Masters in Organizational Development from . . .

Business background: As you know, I am a training consultant with over 20 years of experience in the training and organizational development industry. For the past four years I have been running my own business, and my expertise includes assessing training needs, developing and delivering training solutions, and training internal trainers. My uniqueness is that I am a businessperson first and a trainer second, which means that any training solutions I offer are practical and business-results focused.

Bridge: And the reason I am calling today is . . .

Exercise 6.5 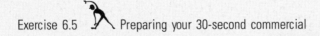 Preparing your 30-second commercial

◆   Take a moment now and create your 30-second commercial. For this exercise, think about a specific upcoming meeting/call so that you can customize the introduction to this specific audience.

Personal: _____

Educational background: _____

Business background: _____

_____

_____

Bridge: _____

Outcome from this meeting/discussion: _____

◆   Now find someone with whom you can try out your 30-second commercial. Ask them particularly to refine the information you have included in education and business background.

◆   Make any further changes below.

Personal: _____

Educational background: _____

Business background: _____

_____

_____

Bridge: _____

Outcome from this meeting/discussion: _____

Coaching point

Initially, it can be very difficult to condense the essence of your services into 30 seconds. The benefit of this process is that it helps you to more clearly articulate what it is you do so that anyone can understand it. The more people who understand it, the more can help you sell it! A great mistake that many consultants make is to 'blind their prospects with science!' so they have no idea what you do or more importantly how you could aid them in their business!

Using the telephone in selling

He conquers who endures.

Persius

Selling, developing and delivering a service such as consulting differs considerably from selling a product like an automobile. These differences pose a special challenge to consultants. How do you make relatively invisible services seem real and useful to prospective clients? This is achieved by making sure the services are understood, and by somehow making them more tangible by talking to and meeting with suspects and prospects.

General guidelines for selling on the telephone

Foul!

Remember, selling by telephone is not the same as 'cold calling'. It involves calling people from your network, suspect and prospect list to obtain ideas and information. If you are effective with contacting people you know, you will never need to make a 'cold call'.

Telephone marketing

Advantages	Disadvantages
◆ Saves time: you can cover many people in a short time. It is an incredibly time-effective tool, particularly in the early stages of business development.	◆ No face-to-face contact: you are not able to see body language cues and therefore it can be harder to build rapport.
◆ Saves money: costs less than travelling to face-to-face meetings.	◆ Difficulty in contact: it is becoming increasingly difficult to talk to 'live' people, instead of message machines.

Telephone marketing requires a concentrated, focused environment, plus rapid evaluation and decision-making. But the benefits can be considerable in terms of increased business.

Time out!

General guidelines on telephone marketing

- ◆ 'Chunk' your time: plan for at least two hours of telephone calls three times a week in the set-up stages of your business and at least two one-hour sessions per week when your business is established.
- ◆ Make sure you utilize your body clock effectively. Telephone marketing is hard work, so make sure if you are a 'lark' (best in the morning) that you make your phone calls then. If you are an 'owl' (best in the afternoon and evening), make your phone calls then.
- ◆ If you are organized, you can make 30–45 calls in a two-to-three hour time frame.
- ◆ Most of the time (approximately 90%) you will be leaving messages on voicemails for the other person. Make sure you leave a specific message including your name and number, the reason you called and a good time to call back.
- ◆ If you are leaving a message on a voicemail, state your name and number at the beginning of the call, and then repeat it again at the end.
- ◆ Don't rush when you repeat your phone number!

♦ Even if you have known the person for a long time, always leave your number. You never know if they have lost their organizer, or if their system has crashed!

♦ Make at least three to five phone calls without giving up. Research was conducted with a sales force. Women were more successful than the men in this study because they made more calls than the men, and many of the decisions to buy took place on the fifth call. Often we take it personally when people do not call us back. Realistically, they are busy, not ignoring us!

♦ If the person still does not return your call, you could send them an email with some information and wait for them to contact you.

♦ Call back every three to five days. On average people return the call, if they are going to, within two to three days.

♦ The ideal use of the telephone in marketing your business would be to make the initial call, send information, and then call again after the information has been received and enough time has passed for the recipient to have read it.

Preparing for a telephone call

As with most work, time spent in preparing and planning can save time when we are actually making calls. Following is a pre-call planning exercise to help you prepare for making contact on the phone.

Exercise 6.6 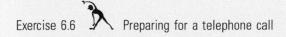 Preparing for a telephone call

♦ Create a mental picture of the person you are contacting and what you both want to accomplish as a result of this phone call.

♦ What do you know about this contact, his/her company and background?

♦ What is your objective in calling?

♦ What questions are you going to ask?

♦ How did you obtain the name of this contact?

♦ Do you understand every conceivable aspect of your background that might be relevant?

◆ What specific questions may this contact ask you, based on your knowledge of him/her?

◆ How can you make sure your voice is pleasant and upbeat?

_____

_____

_____

_____

_____

_____

◆ What were your insights from thinking about the call in this way?

◆ As a result, how will you approach the call differently?

_____

_____

Coaching point

The more you plan, the more prepared and professional you will appear, and the greater the chance of building your business.

Case study: Julia

Julia created her 30-second commercial and tried it out by calling friends and leaving messages with them to obtain feedback on her voice tone, how sincere she sounded and how clear her message was. She initially sent out an email targeted towards start-up companies and then she followed this up by making her first 40 telephone calls. She has been allocating two mornings a week for her telephone marketing efforts. She is using her Palm Pilot to track whom she calls and the responses she is obtaining. She managed to speak to five people directly from those calls, the rest she left a comprehensive message with. Of those five people she managed to talk to directly, every call had a positive outcome. She received four more names of people who might be interested in her services, and she scheduled two meetings. One meeting was with a venture capitalist, who might be able to sub-contract work to her. The other was with a small start-up that might require an HR assessment. Even with the messages she left, she received call-backs from over 40% of the individuals she had called. She sent the two people who gave her names a thank you email.

Managing the telephone interaction

Let's look at the steps in the telephone interaction in a variety of situations for the people from our case studies: when the person is there and it is a good time, when it is not a good time and when there is a voicemail.

Foul!

It can be tempting when you get the person you actually want to talk to on the phone, to jump in immediately with your pitch. Don't!

Always ask 'Is this a good time?' You buy yourself 'Brownie points' and create credibility by so doing. There is nothing worse than picking up a phone and being on the receiving end of a data dump!

As you can see, the first step involves being clear about your expectation for the call, plus being prepared will help you sound confident and organized, which in turn will help to make your contacts feel comfortable helping you.

Person is there and it is a good time: Frank

Step in the call	Person is there: good time
1. Identify purpose for call:	To generate a meeting
2. Short introduction	Hello: This is…We met at the recent Help Desk Institute meeting and you suggested I call you about process reengineering (personal information).
3. Ask for permission	Is this a good time?
4. Introduce purpose and story (30 seconds, two minutes maximum!)	I have a Masters Degree in Quality Engineering (Educational). I have spent the last 20 years both in the field and at corporate headquarters managing and directing technical support operations, working for such organizations as Amdahl, Oracle and IBM. The specific expertise that I bring is that I combine both strategy and process improvement experience, with a practical implementation focus (business background). The reason I am calling today is because we discussed the process-reengineering project you are undertaking and thought I might be able to help (bridge/transition).

5. Transition into questions	What was the driving force behind your process engineering? How far are you into the process? What are the results so far? What is working? Etc.
6. Listen to answers	Make notes as required to act as the basis for more questions. When there is a two-way discussion lasting approximately three to four minutes, transition.
7. Transition	It seems like we might have a fit, in terms of your needs and the services I could provide.
8. Date for a meeting	I will be in your area on ... Is there any time that day that would work for you?

If Frank were calling to try to build his network and/or find advice his bridge would be: 'If you were in my situation, who would you talk to? What would you do? Who else might have ideas?'

Person is there and it is not a good time: Joe

Step in the call	Person is there: not a good time
1. Identify purpose for call:	To ask for advice/information
2. Short introduction with purpose	Hello. This is ... We worked together at Sun, when you were the VP Marketing and I was the Product Manager for ... product. I was calling to see if you could give me any advice as I am setting up my consulting business (personal information).
3. Ask for permission	Is this a good time?
4. Not a good time	When would you like me to try again?
5. Confirm time	So I will call you back at ...
6. Finish call	Thank you and I will look forward to catching up personally then.
7. Call back when promised	If there: continue with purpose, story, questions and summary. If the person is not there, they now have an informal obligation to call you back because you made an appointment and they broke it.

8. Call back three days later if
   don't hear and start again.

Person is not there and you get voicemail: Marie

Step in the call	Person is not there: voicemail
1. Identify purpose for call:	To obtain names
2. Short introduction	Hello. This is ... Linda suggested I call you regarding sales training for your organization.
3. Introduce purpose and story (30 seconds – two minutes maximum!)	I have a Masters Degree in Organizational Development (educational). I recently left ... organization where I was responsible for rolling out sales training to over 5,000 associates in a three month period resulting in a 17% increase in comparative store sales (business background). The reason I am calling today is because Linda suggested that you might need help in training associates at your stores (bridge/transition).
4. Transition into call back	I would be very interested in talking to you about your current sales training process, to discover in what areas I might be able to help you.
5. Give availability	I will be available tomorrow and Friday.
6. Restate contact information	Again, my name is ... And my phone number is ... I look forward to talking personally to you soon.

Coaching point
Be sure to send a thank you note if the person has given you good, useful advice or if he/she has given you a lead. You want to be comfortable calling again if necessary.

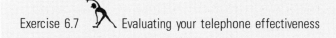

Exercise 6.7 Evaluating your telephone effectiveness

Complete ten to 20 calls to your network and then answer the following questions to assess your effectiveness on the phone.

Yes No

☐ ☐ Were you talking less than 50% of the time in any discussions?

☐ ☐ Were you 100% focused on the other person during the conversations?

☐ ☐ Were you trying to put yourself in the customer's shoes?

☐ ☐ Did you ask questions? Both open and closed?

☐ ☐ Did you let the customer finish what they were saying without interrupting?

☐ ☐ Did you react to the ideas they provided? By repeating or verifying?

☐ ☐ Did you take notes?

☐ ☐ Did you review the notes after the discussion?

☐ ☐ Did you send any follow-up notes/emails?

☐ ☐ Did you make sure the exchange was two-way?

◆ If you answered 'yes' to more than six questions, you are well on the way to building your business by using the telephone effectively. If you answered more than six questions with 'no' you may want to brainstorm ideas to improve the flow of conversation.

◆ What can you do to improve your telephone effectiveness?

_____

_____

Coaching point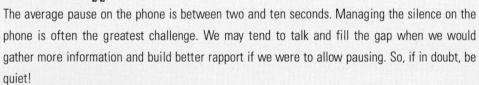

The average pause on the phone is between two and ten seconds. Managing the silence on the phone is often the greatest challenge. We may tend to talk and fill the gap when we would gather more information and build better rapport if we were to allow pausing. So, if in doubt, be quiet!

As you can see, managing the telephone interaction is critical to optimizing your business success. However many people feel uncomfortable about contacting others for information or for ideas. By being clear about your purpose and examining reasons for your reluctance, you can overcome this obstacle.

Just do it!!

Courtesy of Nike

Managing the sales meeting

Now that we have looked at real-time interaction on the phone, let's review some techniques used to manage the face-to-face sales meeting.

Time out!
Managing the sales meeting:
S: start the interaction positively
E: engage the client: ask open-ended questions, listen, and paraphrase
L: list features and benefits that relate to the client's needs
L: leave with the next step planned.

Let's look at these steps in a little more detail.

S: start the interaction positively

Time out!
Remember, when you meet prospects for the first time, the factors that influence your communication are:
◆ body language (55%) (includes eye contact, gestures, facial expression, etc)
◆ the way you say the words (38%) (includes tone, delivery, enunciation, pausing, filler words, etc)
◆ the word choice (7%) (includes vocabulary and word choice),

Step S	Guidelines
Start the interaction	◆ Positively provide a professional greeting: handshake and eye contact.
	◆ Build rapport by small-talk and mirroring body language and delivery.
	◆ Establish credibility by talking about the company/ current events.
	◆ Exchange business cards.
	◆ Can last any time from one minute to ten depending on the client.

- The client will let you know when they are ready to move on by providing some type of body language cue e.g. they will pick up a pen, sit forward, or move somehow.
- The need for this stage is larger at the beginning of the relationship because it takes time to build trust.

Foul!

If you miss the body language clue that the client is ready to move on to the next stage of the interaction, the prospective client may then ask you to describe your services and you will not know the specific needs that the client wishes to be addressed.

E: engage the client

The critical point in selling a service is to identify client needs and objectives before you begin to describe your products or services. Clients will only commit to purchasing services when they are convinced that the consultant's support will help them meet their business objectives. The chances for closing a sale are greater if you actively search out the customer's needs. But more importantly, clients will feel more valued if the consultant takes an active interest in their business.

Time out!

There are two ways of uncovering client needs: making assumptions, and asking questions.
Making assumptions: can be risky – makes an ASS out of U and ME.
Asking questions: should be primarily open-ended questions. Open-ended questions cannot be answered 'yes' or 'no'.

| **Step E: Engage the client**
Asking open-ended questions | **Guidelines**
◆ This part of the sales interaction can last over 20 minutes, with many open-ended questions being asked.
◆ Use phrases such as 'tell me about, describe and explain' to act as excellent topic-opener statements to begin a subject area.
◆ Use 'who, what, when, where, why and how' as open-ended questions to probe and gather more information.
◆ Use closed questions to gather specific data or move to |

the next stage of the interaction.

◆ Think about the client's current business situation, overall business goals and specific challenges in the area where you can provide help.

◆ Begin with general questions, in terms of business challenges, and become more specific, focusing on the areas in which you can provide a service.

◆ Ask as many questions as you can, until you have gathered enough information or until the client is ready to move on to finding out about you and your services.

◆ At the end of this chapter is a general list of questions that can be used to gather information about the business.

Listen actively

◆ Take notes to help you listen.

◆ Concentrate on the other person and pay attention to what they are saying and what else might be going on.

◆ Be patient with the silence of if they do not talk as quickly as you do!

◆ Remember the influence in a sales interaction goes to the listener not the speaker.

◆ Make sure you listen by observing body language clues – that blank look is a good indicator that the client has no idea what you are talking about.

◆ Don't rehearse what you will say as the other person is talking. Make sure you stay focused on the other person.

◆ Don't prematurely jump to conclusions – let the person finish talking and keep listening.

Paraphrasing

◆ Paraphrasing involves repeating back to the client in your own words, what they have just told you.

◆ Don't repeat word for word – that's parroting and can be viewed as patronizing.

◆ Don't provide your judgment or opinion, just a neutral restatement of what they said to you.

◆ Paraphrasing has many benefits, which include:
  – validating the client
  – checking for understanding between what you heard and they said
  – gives you time to think about the next questions.

When the prospective client's posture changes, this is the time to begin to describe the products and services that you can offer that will meet their needs.

Case study: engaging the client – questioning is key

Marie was meeting with a client and at the beginning of the meeting the client asked, 'Do you do cultural diversity training?' Marie did not, but she said, 'That's an interesting question, why is this subject important?' To her surprise, the client began to describe the environment and the training needs, which encompassed entry level management training for a supervisory group who mainly originated from Vietnam. By understanding the broader business context by asking questions, listening and paraphrasing, Marie was able to define a service that she offered, management training with some emphasis on dealing with different cultures. The client did not want intense cultural training.

L: list features and benefits that relate to the client's needs

Step L	**Guidelines**
List features relating to client needs	◆ Position the services you offer in terms of the features and benefits you determined in Chapter 5. The benefits will relate directly to the needs you have identified in the sales meeting.
Ask for status	◆ If you are not sure where you are in the process and you observe a change in posture, the best thing you can do is to ask the client one of the following four questions: how does that sound? how does this information look? what do you think? how do you feel about this information?

Foul!

This is the step in the sales interaction when the business can be sold or lost. Many consultants fail to watch the body language clues from the client as they describe their service's features and benefits. As a result they continue to talk and walk straight into and out of the sale. If we miss that critical moment when the client wishes to buy, then we may not be able to close the sale. Over half of sales are lost because the critical cues from the customer are missed.

L: leave with the next step

Often the end of the interaction does not mean the closing of the sale. When selling services, on average, it takes two to three appointments to close the sale. However, it is necessary to ensure that when you leave you have the critical next steps identified so that you do not have to revisit the voicemail endless cycle! The next steps could include:

◆ a further meeting with other decision makers and influencers
◆ sending a proposal
◆ a formal presentation to senior management.

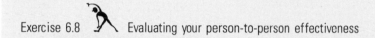

Exercise 6.8   Evaluating your person-to-person effectiveness

◆ Complete a visit with a prospective client with a colleague. Brief him/her on the steps you will be trying to adhere to in the sales cycle.

◆ Make sure you position the additional person in the meeting with the client as a colleague from your consulting team.

◆ After the meeting, discuss the following questionnaire with him/her to identify what went well and what else could have increased the success of the meeting.

Step in the sales meeting	Questions
S: start the interaction	◆ How long did this step in the interaction take? ◆ How well did the consultant greet the client? ◆ How did the consultant build rapport? ◆ To what extent did the consultant talk about the client's business in the introduction? ◆ To what extent did the consultant pay attention to the client's body language and transition into gathering information about needs?
E: engage the client	◆ How long did this stage of the interaction last? ◆ How many open-ended questions did the consultant ask? ◆ How many closed questions? ◆ How well did the consultant listen to the client's needs? ◆ How did you know that he/she was listening? ◆ How well, if at all, did the consultant paraphrase the information gathered?

| | ◆ What other information could the consultant have obtained which would have aided in the sales process? |

L: list features and benefits

◆ How long did this stage in the interaction last?
◆ How clear was the consultant about the benefits of his/her services?
◆ To what extent were these services linked to client needs?
◆ How alert was the consultant to changes in posture?
◆ Did the consultant ask for status: How does that sound? Look? Feel? What do you think?
◆ How effectively did the consultant manage any concerns expressed?

L: leave with the next step planned

◆ How long did this stage of the interaction last?
◆ To what extent did the consultant confirm next steps?
◆ What else could the consultant have done to increase the chances of a sale?

◆ Based on this discussion, what can you do to improve your sales effectiveness in a meeting?

_____

_____

_____

Coaching point

The more you can adhere to these steps and get feedback, the greater the chance of building a successful consulting business. Don't be afraid to use a coach to guide you in this process.

Adjusting your style to maximize sales

We don't see things as they are, we see things as we are.

Anais Nin

As we discussed in Chapter 2, each of us may view the world slightly differently based on our temperament. This becomes increasingly important in the sales process, where clients from differing temperaments will communicate differently and look for different benefits.

Below is a table highlighting the different communication style associated with each temperament.

The four languages of temperament

Area	Artisan	Guardian	Rational	Idealist
Subjects	Concrete data: practical and tangible around action	Concrete data: practical and tangible around process and results	Abstract data: around theories and systems	Abstract data: around people and their needs
Structure	Tactical and to the point: 1,2,3...net it out	Linear and sequential: 1, 1.1, 1.2, 2, 2.1, 2.2, 2.2a, 2.2b	Strategic: categorized under headings	Interconnected around a central theme
Words	Colloquial language: jargon, slang, short and to the point Similes and stories	Traditional language: respectful and considered Examples from experience	Precise language: sophisticated and elaborate words Analogies and metaphors	Global language: over-exaggeration of data Analogies and metaphors
Delivery	Fast-paced	Structured	Deliberate	Flowing and dramatic
Body language/ gestures	Clawing with hands	Finger pointing and chopping	Pull ideas from the air	Circles with hands and open gestures
Body language	May appear casual and unprofessional	May appear deliberate and formal	May appear distant and preoccupied	May appear warm and gushing
Humour	Outrageous or physical	Dry: tongue in cheek, sarcastic	Cerebral: double meanings, words and puns	Use personal examples and self-deprecating jokes
Questioning style	Questioning on motive	Questioning to identify relevant experience	Questioning of theories and competence	Questioning to find what's important to the person
Filter information based on	What is this person's relevant experience?	What is this person's past experience and skill set?	How competent and knowledgeable is this person?	How does this person approach others?

Based on these differing styles, here are a few ideas for improving the sales interaction with each temperament.

Communicating with Artisans

◆ Use short and more direct communication.

◆ Remember – less is more.

◆ Talk about concrete realities.

◆ Get to the point quickly and keep moving.

◆ Expect cynicism and stories.

◆ Adapt to their colloquial language.

◆ Use tools and hands-on experiences when explaining approaches.

◆ Talk about impact, end results and variety.

◆ Remember, they read body language very accurately so watch your body language cues.

Communicating with Guardians

◆ Talk about what was done in the past and your prior experience.

◆ Explain concrete, practical implementation approach.

◆ Be specific about who is responsible for what in terms of roles and responsibilities.

◆ Explain steps sequentially, starting at the beginning and using numbering 1,2,3,4,5.

◆ Be specific about the expected results.

◆ Expect questions about 'rules', 'what can be done' and 'what cannot be done'.

◆ Focus on efficiencies and process improvements.

◆ Provide lots of data and background information.

◆ Give practical examples.

Communicating with Rationals

◆ Start with the big picture.

◆ Use precise language when explaining concepts and ideas.

◆ Make sure of your facts and present theoretical information where possible. Don't bluff!

◆ Expect critical questioning to clarify a point of view.

◆ Recognize their intellectual competence.

◆ Talk about your expertise in a specific field.

- Use analogies to make points.
- Attend to the conditional language 'if this … then …'.
- Always explain what and why.

Communicating with Idealists

- Talk about the purpose of an approach.
- Be authentic when communicating – they will pick up 'fake' conversation.
- Focus on the big picture and conceptual ideas.
- Use metaphors and analogies.
- Talk about the benefits to people of actions: ability to develop potential and the 'greater good'.
- Don't provide too much practical detail.
- Listen to their insights on people, which is usually accurate.
- Build an empathetic relationship.

Writing successful proposals

Defeat is not the worst of failures. Not to have tried is the true failure.

George E. Woodberry

Many appointments result in a client's request for a proposal.

Time out!
A proposal is usually a document you write for the client that:
- Describes your understanding of the client's need.
- Paraphrases the key information gathered in the meeting(s) with the client and restates what the client requested.
- States what you intend to do for the client.
- Indicates what anticipated results and potential benefits the client will gain as a consequence of the engagement.
- Outlines your approach and qualifications.
- Tries to persuade the client to accept your proposal.

Foul!

Don't get caught by clients who say, without having met you, 'Send me a proposal and then we can discuss it'. This is classic avoidance behaviour from the client.

1. You don't know their needs so how can you send a proposal?
2. You will only spend time creating something generic and they will reply 'This is not what we are looking for!'

The complexity of the proposal will depend on the size of the project and type of consulting that you do. Remember that the proposal needs to include critical information, but should not be over cumbersome.

Below are listed some sample areas:

Item	Explanation
Table of contents	Only for long, complex proposals
Background information	Include a summary of the background information that you have gathered in the meetings. Will normally include detail about the company, the current business environment, current challenges and key people involved.
Purpose	Purpose of the proposed engagement.
Objectives	A description of the key outcomes that you expect from the consulting assignment. It may also include details on critical deliverables.
Approach	A description of the critical steps and methodologies that will be used in the consulting assignment, the scope of the project and a plan.
Content	Key areas in which service will be provided.
Pricing summary	Compensation amount expected for the critical steps: see Chapter 7 for more information about rates. This will also include payment terms and cancellation rates.
Progress checks	For longer-term projects, this will include information about interim progress reports, deliverables and critical milestones in the project.
Qualifications	If this is the first time you have worked with the client you may need to include a summary of qualifications, client list and possible references.

Resources	Again, if this is a large contract, include a definition of other consultants to be used.
Responsibilities	A listing of your responsibilities and the clients'.

Coaching points

◆ Be sure to not give away too much information in your proposal. Give only enough to make the prospective client want to come back and ask for more. If you provide too much advice and/or data, the client may decide to do the work themselves.

◆ It is not generally a good idea to send a generic proposal. You need to meet and spend time with the prospective client in order to understand as much as possible what his/her needs are, then the proposal can be specifically tuned to those needs. (Since it is sometimes impossible to actually meet, this step may be done on the telephone, but a face-to-face meeting is always preferable.)

◆ A proposal should not take more than two to four hours to prepare. One to two is optimal.

◆ When facing competition for a project, remember this rule: someone always has the inside track. Consultants refer to this as being 'wired'. The first question you need to ask yourself then is if you have the inside track. Is there someone within the organization who will push for you and keep you in the running? Try to keep these key people on your side. Competitors also have sponsors who are usually different from yours. You can estimate your chances of getting the assignment by comparing the power of your sponsor *vs.* the power of competitors' sponsors. Under certain circumstances you will not have the inside track but you should bid anyway because this may provide a chance for person-to-person exposure to the client. More importantly, the client may also have future projects, and if impressed with you, he or she may engage you for them.

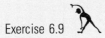

Exercise 6.9   Deciding your proposal approach

◆ Review the list on the previous page and decide, for your area of consulting, which categories you would select.

◆ Talk to three other consultants in a similar field to you and ask them (or get a copy if possible) what they include in their proposals. What type of information? What format? What ideas could you include in your proposals?

_____

_____

◆ Now spend some time creating a standard template for a proposal so that it is easier to build in the specific client information.

Presenting the proposal

It is normally preferable to ask to present your proposal in person. This serves two purposes.

◆ It indicates how serious you are about the client and their project.
◆ A presentation in person increases your chances of clinching the sale.

After presenting the proposal, you will want some indication the client has selected you as a consultant. You must take the initiative to finalize the sale. You close the sale by simply asking or by estimating when you are going to start. Once the client chooses you as a consultant, send him or her a letter of understanding to confirm your arrangement.

Using cover letters

If you do not personally present your proposal, or if you are unable to contact the prospective client by phone, it is often a good idea to send a cover letter with the proposal or with the information about your services. Cover letters are used to:

◆ build rapport with the client
◆ introduce your objective for contacting them
◆ reaffirm information you know about the client
◆ outline your qualifications
◆ ask for a close.

> Time out!
> A cover letter should include the following information:
> *Reason for writing*: article, referral, advertisement, research, previous meeting.

Summary of services: brief overview of range of services and experience.

Summary of perceived need: the need they may have based on your previous information, and how you could help them meet that need.

Close: ask for the next steps, whether it is an appointment, a phone conversation or a confirmation.

What if the client says no?

Success consists of going from failure to failure without loss of enthusiasm.

Sir Winston Churchill

The most difficult part of sales involves when the client says no.

Time out!

Here are a few guidelines to help you manage the inevitable emotion that these negative answers might generate:

◆   The more clients who say 'no', the greater the chances that one will say 'yes'.

◆   If the service is not the right fit, it is better not to get the work than to do it and fail.

◆   Use this as an opportunity to evaluate your sales effectiveness. Is there something that you missed? What else could you have done?

◆   They are not rejecting you personally, they are saying 'no' to your services currently. Who knows what future opportunities there might be with this client?

◆   Make sure you handle the negative response in a professional manner – this increases the chance that the client will come back to you again if they have further needs.

What if the client says yes?

Success is how high you bounce when you hit bottom.

General George S. Patton

Congratulations, your first major milestone has been achieved. Now you have to make sure the client pays you and you complete the work successfully. Keep reading for more tips!

Sample questions to ask

Foul!

Don't ask all the questions! Select the ones that are most relevant for your particular client!

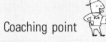

Coaching point

Obviously the more information you can have at your finger tips before the client meeting the better. You can then use questioning to deepen your knowledge within specific areas.

General business

♦ What is the revenue of the company?
♦ How many years has the company been in business?
♦ Who founded the company?
♦ Is either the founder or starter team still active in the business?
♦ What has been the sales growth in the past year? Two years? Etc?
♦ What are the company's top five corporate goals? (Increase market share, enhance quality, improve client satisfaction, control costs, increase profitability, etc.)
♦ What needs to be enhanced or accomplished by the company to achieve these goals?
♦ What are the greatest business challenges/problems that are a priority to address in the next six to 12 months?
♦ Who does the company consider to be their most serious competitors? How would any competitor compare or contrast your company or approach to theirs?
♦ What will the company look like two to three years from now?
♦ What external influences are of greatest consequence to the corporation?
♦ What is the financial structure of the company?
♦ What is the outstanding debt of the company?
♦ Is the company public?

- In the history of the company, what were the biggest advance and the biggest s
- What does the client see as the strengths and weaknesses of this company?

Marketing and customers

- What significant market opportunities or threats will the company face over the next 3–5 years?
- What primary and secondary markets is the company currently targeting?
- How many different customers does the company have?
- Who are the organization's customers? Local, regional, national or international?
- What is the profile of the ideal customer?
- What restructuring or expansions are planned over the next year or two?
- What is the most profitable line of business and what are the development plans for this line?
- What market segment is the organization part of?
- How is the industry structured?
- What is the organization's role in the way the industry is structured?
- What is unique about the way the company competes?
- What is the company's specific market niche?
- What promotional strategies are used within this market niche?
- How is the industry outlook?
- What are the plans to expand to new market areas?

Organization

- Who does what in the organization?
- What are the main functions in the organization?
- What is the highest priority in the next six months and how could you help?
- How is the budgeting process managed?
- In addition to revenue, what else is monitored on a regular basis?
- What companies, departments, divisions or sites make up the corporate structure? How are they related?
- How are the products/services organized within that structure?
- How centralized or decentralized are operational and profit/loss responsibilities?
- What is the reporting structure for the client's function?

Culture questions

- What key values does the firm consider important? How are these communicated throughout the organization?
- What does the company have written about its culture? In terms of annual reports, quarterly statement, brochures?
- Can all individuals state the company's mission or reason for being? Do individuals have a clear picture of its values?
- What are the slogans in the organization?
- How do beliefs affect the day-to-day business of the organization?
- What are the stories in the organization?
- How is the physical environment?
- What are the rites and rituals present in the organization? How are high performers recognised? What are the opportunities for team recognition? What are the team activities supported by the company?
- How are meetings managed? (If possible, try to attend a meeting.) How often are meetings held? For the team? For individuals? How do employees get involved in meetings? Where do people sit?
- What is the company's compensation philosophy?
- What is the company's training philosophy?
- How are new employees hired and introduced to the company?
- What awards are given in the organization? What values do these awards reinforce?
- Are there language rituals, such as the extensive use of jargon? How are individuals addressed?
- What are the unwritten rules of behaviour in the organization? E.g. Nepotism? Sexist jokes? Dress code?
- Are there predefined standards for presentation of materials?
- How and when are memos used in the organization?
- Who are the heroes of the organization? Why are they recognised as such? What does this demonstrate about the culture?
- What are people like who work at the organization? How long have they been there? What is the staff turnover rate?
- How do you feel about the president or CEO? What do you recognise about his or her temperament?
- How are strangers greeted in the organization?
- What is the format of the average day?

- What is the company's strategic planning process?
- What are the main communication channels? Formal or informal?
- How do these communication channels work?
- How are decisions made in the company? Is there a formal chain of command for decisions? How far does the president delegate decision-making?

Current environment questions

- What current challenges are facing the business?
- What is being done to address the challenges?
- What changes have taken place in the past few months?

Checklist

Have you:

- Written down the benefits to you of selling?
- Highlighted in your database your 40–50 suspects?
- Picked out any interesting prospects?
- Created your introductory commercial?
- Decided who will be the first 20 people you will contact?
- Identified the outcome you require from these 20 calls?
- Fixed three meetings with influencers, decision-makers and prospects?
- Created a list of questions to ask prospects?
- Practised paraphrasing and probing for specifics?
- Created a template for proposals?

Scorecard

Before moving on to Chapter 7, think about the following questions:

- In terms of the sales process, what tools and techniques will you use to ensure that you are conducting activities in all of the critical stages in business development: network, suspects, prospects, proposals and clients. How long do you believe the sales process is for your type of business? How many people do you think you need in each category to be successful?

◆ How many telephone calls do you think would be appropriate for your type of business? How will you ensure that you are practising the key skills when making telephone calls? What is the target you will set yourself and how will you measure your success?

◆ What meetings will you schedule? How will you ensure that you are using these meetings to gather information and not just talk? How can you practise asking open-ended questions and listening? What type of proposal is required for your business?

SECTION THREE:
Getting Money

CHAPTER SEVEN

Financing Your Business

Game plan

The area of obtaining funding, establishing fee rates and collecting your outstanding accounts receivable is often one of the most misunderstood, and underestimated, areas of your consulting business.

The purpose of this chapter is to help you to:

- Create a realistic estimate of start-up costs.
- Evaluate and obtain funding to begin your consulting business.
- Establish financial objectives to guide your efforts.
- Build a revenue and cash flow statement for your business to ensure financial liquidity.
- Decide your fee structure and rates to maximize potential revenue.
- Manage your accounts receivable so that you limit bad debts and protect cash flow.
- Understand the financial infrastructure inherent in sub-contracting.
- Provide the basis and infrastructure for achieving a profitable consulting business.

Estimating your start-up and ongoing costs

> Money is like manure. You have to spread it around or it smells!
>
> *J. Paul Getty*

Every business faces one-time start-up costs, which are dependent on the type of consulting you are doing, your location and your plans. Often it is easy to overlook these start-up costs, particularly if you have been working at a large company where they are part of the infrastructure. It is important also to plan systematically for all monthly expenses. The following is a checklist of possible areas of cost:

☐ Car/insurance	☐ Rent	☐ Office preparation	☐ Computer hardware
☐ Cable connections/ internet access fees	☐ Telephone/mobile phone/fax	☐ Other office equipment and furniture	☐ Computer software
☐ Utilities	☐ Postage	☐ Stationery and business cards	☐ Insurance
☐ Printing and supplies	☐ Answering service	☐ Typing services	☐ Accounting and legal services
☐ Business licenses and permits	☐ Advertising and promotion	☐ Dues and subscriptions	☐ Books and reference materials
☐ Travel	☐ Conventions	☐ Continuing education	☐ Entertainment
☐ Gifts	☐ Salaries	☐ Unemployment insurance	☐ Eating out

Time out!

As you are starting your business, the two areas of cost that tend to be immediately higher than the others are your phone bill and eating out expenses. When you first begin marketing your business, as we discussed in Chapters 5 and 6, the telephone becomes a time-effective business development tool. You might expect, depending on your speed and proficiency on the phone, for your phone bill to at least double in the early months. In addition, much of the time you spend with networking contacts will be over food of some kind – breakfast, coffee, lunch, dinner, etc!

Foul!

Consultants are often tempted to pick up the bill when eating out, because now it is a deductible expense. However, as any accountant would say, 'Don't spend money to save money!' Try to minimize eating out – meetings are often more productive when held separately from meals.

Exercise 7.1   What are your start-up costs and estimated monthly expenses?

Thinking about your consulting business, look at the list opposite and fill in the table below with your estimates of start-up costs and possible monthly expenses.

Category	Start-up costs	Monthly expenses
Office space and furniture		
Computer hardware and software		
Telephones/mobile phones/fax		
Travel and expenses		
Meals		
Advertising		
Marketing/collateral		
Stationery and postage		
Conferences/continuing education		
Insurances		
Car		
Vendors/services		
Owners' draw/salary		

- ◆ Looking at the amount above, what costs are essential? How could you save costs in the start-up phase?

Coaching point

It can be too easy for start-up costs to get out of control. By creating a realistic estimate of these costs and your approximate monthly outgoings, you will be in a better position to manage your business. More information on setting up your office is included in Section Four.

Case study: Marie

Marie already has a computer at home, but she knows her main start-up cost will be eating out and phone calls. The first time she was a consultant her telephone bill trebled and eating out doubled. This time, she has decided to try to have meetings separately from meals, but is prepared for the rise in the phone calls, as she believes this is a critical start-up cost for her.

Did you know that . . .

◆ the average cost of setting up a business has increased in real terms since 1990 with today's average start-up cost being £17,680;

◆ equipment is the biggest single expenses – 44%;

according to Barclays 'Starting up in Business'.

Funding your business in the start-up phase

Money may kindle, but it cannot by itself, and for very long, burn.

Igor Stravinski

It is important to have a certain amount of money in reserve to live on while your business gets started for a variety of reasons.

◆ To cover the start-up costs and early monthly expense requirements.

◆ In case you get sick and can't work for any amount of time, or if someone close to you becomes ill and you need to care for them.

◆ Most importantly so that you do not appear desperate when selling. You will sell more effectively if you're not too hungry. If you are too eager, the customer may pick up on it and wonder if you're good enough.

Let's look at how we can fund our business in this start-up phase.

Time out!

◆ You need a minimum of six months' living money, but it is optimum to have one year. Why? It takes time to close your first contract: minimally six weeks, can be as much as six months.

◆ Often it is necessary to complete some consulting work for a period of time before you can invoice, particularly as you are getting started and have less credibility.

◆ Finally, most companies pay invoices four to eight weeks after they are received: the average time is six weeks.

Identifying sources of capital

Once you have calculated your profit and loss and cash flow statement (see page 159), and estimated your start-up costs, you should be able to calculate how much income you need in order to resource your business. There are various options for funding your business.

Type	Comments
A bank loan	When dealing with a bank you should provide the business plan, look the part, and be prepared to shop around for a bank to back you. Many established banks are still reluctant to fund new business ventures.
Friends/venture capital	More often than you might suspect, you can find friends who believe in your undertaking more than your banker. Also, there is a range of venture capital firms that will often finance new businesses. People with venture capital often want a greater portion of the company ownership. In addition, there are some entrepreneurs who will fund start-ups.
Your savings	More often than not, your personal savings are adequate to finance your start-up as a consultant. You will need approximately a year's worth of income as a back-up resource.

Selling shares	You may consider selling some shares of stock to finance your start.
Redundancy packages	You may use funds received from your previous company when laid off.
Credit cards	Many people with service businesses have financed themselves with credit cards since this has been the only credit available to them. Bear in mind that this is the most expensive way to finance since most credit card companies charge very high interest rates. However many credit cards offer low introductory rates and will help consolidate your previous debt. For example, the founder of a consulting organization who was 36, had three children under 12, and was the main breadwinner, funded his start-up business with credit cards. The business ultimately grossed 20 million pounds, with 25% net profit – he definitely covered his credit card bills!
Equity line of credit	Many banks and financial institutions will offer equity lines of credit on a primary property, which can be used to fund business growth. It is important to obtain this line of credit *before* you begin your business. It is more difficult after you start your business and/or lose your full-time income.
The moonlighting plan	Keep your full-time job and develop your business as a sideline. When it takes off you can go full-time. But be sure to work at least eight hours a week on the sideline business. Obviously the challenges inherent in this approach are the overall hours you will need to work, combined with the limited hours you will be able to invest in your business.
The part-time plan	Work at a part-time job to provide a base income while you are building up the business. When your business equals the base income, drop the part-time job. Again, you may face similar challenges to those listed above, but it can help to at least cover base expense requirements.
The spin-off plan	Turn your previous employer into your first major client, or, when ethically possible, take a major client with you from your previous job. Be aware though that some organizations will place limitations on the extent to

which this is possible. For instance IBM now will not take back previous employees as sub-contractors within the first year. Many organizations therefore have arisen who then act as a broker between the client and the prior employee to avoid this limitation.

The piggyback plan

If you have a working spouse or partner, cut back on your expenses and live on one salary until the business gets going.

Borrow from retirement funds

It is possible to borrow against retirement funds. The challenge with this is that there are often penalties for early withdrawal, but on the other side, if you can invest the money in your consulting business, you will probably be able to get a larger return in the long run and pay for future funds.

Case studies: finding funds

Joe talked with his company about his need for new challenge, and this coincided with their need to reduce costs. However they did not want to lose Joe's expertise completely, so they were able to structure a contract where he worked on one major project, on a consulting basis, with them for the next three months. It proved to be a win–win: Joe obtained a stream of revenue for three months, and a client, while his company saved costs yet retained the talent for the project that they required.

Frank has extended the equity line of credit on his house, and has six months in savings behind him.

Julia had the easiest decision to make: she owned shares in a company where she had worked that went public. She sold enough to cover a year with no revenue.

Exercise 7.2 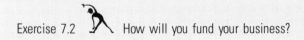 How will you fund your business?

Thinking about your consulting business, answer the questions below to help you to evaluate funding options for your business.

◆ In Exercise 7.1 what did you calculate your costs and expenses needs to be?

♦ Looking at the sources of funds above, what is your best way of covering these costs?

_____

_____

♦ What will you do, by when, to obtain this funding?

Action	What	Who	When	Completed
1				
2				
3				

Coaching point

By spending time sourcing funds in an organized way, you will not only reduce your stress level, but will also ensure you have the resources necessary to support you while you are building your business.

Establishing financial objectives

You need to establish financial goals for your business within the **finance key result area**. Again, these goals need to meet SMART criteria as outlined by Allen Lakein. They need to be:

S – specific
M – measurable
A – aligned
R – results-focused
T – time-based.

Exercise 7.3   Establishing financial objectives

Thinking about your consulting business, create objectives on a separate sheet of paper using the information below:

Category
Objectives and things to consider

Overall sales revenue	Total gross revenue figure you would like to generate. Remember this is not the same as profit – see next section for more information.
Profit	Figure left after expenses are paid.
Fee structure	Target fee amount and/or number of projects. This may overlap with the sales objectives described in Chapter 6.
Aging percentage	Targets for 30 days, 45 days and 60 days.
Cash flow	Target cash balance below which you will not allow your account to go.

Case study: Joe

Joe listed the following two financial objectives:

To achieve revenue of £.... in financial year ending 31 December 200X.

This was the same amount as the salary he had received for full time employment. He knew that he would have to pay expenses out of this amount but he thought this would provide enough income to cover costs and a lower living standard.

To have 100% of revenue collected from clients within 60 days with 0% bad debts.

He knew this would require focus, but he thought this was essential for maintaining his cash flow.

Setting clear objectives for the financial side of your business will help to ensure that you make your business successful and viable.

Creating revenue statements

In managing business performance, there are two critical financial reports: the **revenue statement** and **cash flow statement**. Let's look at the details in the revenue statement first. It shows the monthly invoice amount and costs.

Revenue

When you are getting started, based on your business plan, calculate your estimated revenue for the first year that will include all income from your business. If your business is already operating, the revenue figure will comprise the total of your invoices.

Example
For instance: if you wish to invoice £600 a day, and you budget on working 10 days a month, your revenue figure will be £6,000 each month.

Month	Jan	Feb	Mar	Apr	May	June	July	Aug	Sept	Oct	Nov	Dec
Consulting income	6,000	6,000	6,000	6,000	6,000	6,000	6,000	6,000	6,000	6,000	6,000	6,000
Mat	500	500	500	500	500	500	500	500	500	500	500	500
Rev	6,500	6,500	6,500	6,500	6,500	6,500	6,500	6,500	6,500	6,500	6,500	6,500

In addition you may have other income from materials and sales of products. Each will be budgeted in the month the sale takes place, not necessarily when the income comes in.

Costs

Your costs will include sales, marketing, salaries, rent, equipment, utilities and so on as listed in the earlier section.

Time out!
Costs are broken down into fixed costs, which are costs which will occur whether or not there are sales e.g. utilities, cost of your car and office rental, and variable costs which are costs you would not have incurred if you had not made a sale e.g. printing of materials, shipping and phone calls.

Costs	Jan	Feb	Mar	Apr	May	June	July	Aug	Sept	Oct	Nov	Dec
Car	250	250	250	250	250	250	250	250	250	250	250	250
Rent	500	500	500	500	500	500	500	500	500	500	500	500
Mat	250	250	250	250	250	250	250	250	250	250	250	250
Phone	250	250	250	250	250	250	250	250	250	250	250	250
Costs	**1,250**	**1,250**	**1,250**	**1,250**	**1,250**	**1,250**	**1,250**	**1,250**	**1,250**	**1,250**	**1,250**	**1,250**

Profit/loss

After you add up all your costs and subtract them from your sales, you have your profit/loss. Profits are usually stated as a percentage of your total sales revenue.

Month	Jan	Feb	Mar	Apr	May	June	July	Aug	Sept	Oct	Nov	Dec
Rev	6,500	6,500	6,500	6,500	6,500	6,500	6,500	6,500	6,500	6,500	6,500	6,500
Costs	1,250	1,250	1,250	1,250	1,250	1,250	1,250	1,250	1,250	1,250	1,250	1,250
Profit	5,250	5,250	5,250	5,250	5,250	5,250	5,250	5,250	5,250	5,250	5,250	5,250
%age	80%	80%	80%	80%	80%	80%	80%	80%	80%	80%	80%	80%

Many small companies now use computer-based software to help them manage the financial side of the business. Quick Books is currently the market leader in this area.

Creating cash flow statements

The cash flow analysis explains the amount and timing of expected cash in flows and out flows.

Time out!
The cash flow statement is usually divided into the sources of the funds and the uses to which the funds are put. Sources of funds normally include sales revenue, owner investment, loans and

outside equity investment. Use of funds is typically expenditures for rent, salaries, equipment, taxes, and interests on loans and other costs.

The purpose of the cash flow analysis is to determine if you will have enough in-coming sources of funds to meet required out-going uses. In the previous example, if all else remains constant, yet we use cash flow statements to manage the financial side of the business, you can see the difference in the example below.

Month	Jan	Feb	Mar	Apr	May	June	July	Aug	Sept	Oct	Nov	Dec
Cash			6,500	6,500	6,500	6500	6,500	6,500	6,500	6,500	6,500	6,500
Costs	1,250	1,250	1,250	1,250	1,250	1,250	1,250	1,250	1,250	1,250	1,250	1,250
Profit	-1,250	-1,250	5,250	5,250	5,250	5,250	5,250	5,250	5,250	5,250	5,250	5,250
%age			80%	80%	80%	80%	80%	80%	80%	80%	80%	80%

In this example, we are assuming that the consulting work performed in January is invoiced in January, but that payment does not take place until 60 days later. We are also assuming that the costs to be paid in March can wait until the revenue is received. More likely, many of the March costs would have to be paid before that income is received. As you can see, with steady income and a 60-day payment term, you will not only have to pay the monthly costs for two months, but you will also not have any cash coming in to pay any other home or living expenses.

Foul!

More businesses fail due to lack of cash than lack of revenue so most consultants use the cash-in/cash-out approach to managing their business.

Case study: Susan

Susan had too much work for her to manage, and when she reviewed her workload she decided that she could afford to pay a sub-contractor full-time for three months. However, when she began the work she discovered that she had to pay her sub-contractor immediately, but that she would not receive the income until three months later, and as a result had to use money from her savings to absorb the cost.

Exercise 7.4 Creating your cash flow statement

◆ Fill in your estimated revenue projections in the revenue row.
◆ Fill in your estimated expenses in the costs column.

Month	Jan	Feb	Mar	Apr	May	June	July	Aug	Sept	Oct	Nov	Dec
Cash												
Costs												
Profit												

◆ What shortfall did you notice? Were the funds you raised in Exercise 7.2 sufficient to cover your cash flow for the first six months?

_____

_____

◆ How else could you generate funds?

_____

_____

Coaching point

While these exercises might appear tedious, they are essential to establishing your business on a sound footing. Persevere!

Setting your billing rate

Money is the most egalitarian force in society. It confers power on whoever holds it.

Roger Starr

When people who are not consultants hear a billing rate, they often see the figure as astronomically high because they compare it to the salary they are earning, if it was paid on an hourly basis. Unfortunately, this is not a fair comparison as the consultant's rate includes many factors that are included above and beyond the employee's salary.

Considerations

The consulting fees charged are your revenue and it is important when setting a billing rate to take into consideration the following nine items.

Factors	Considerations
Salary	This is your worth as a labour commodity on the open market performing the same services you provide as a consultant.
Research and development	This is an important overhead expense in time and money, which is often forgotten. This includes purchasing books, finding answers to questions, taking classes, purchasing new software, etc. As you continue to improve your skills or streamline your operations, this cost needs to be covered in your consulting fee.
Employee benefits	Benefits are the extras you receive from an employer, above and beyond your salary, which are often tax-free. For most employees, benefits amount to 25–60% of their salary and include such items as insurance, training, holiday, sick leave, pension, unemployment insurance and payroll taxes. In addition, employers often match employees' contributions in factors such as retirement plans, medical coverage, etc. The consulting rate has to cover all the benefit costs.
Overhead expenses	Overhead represents the expenses incurred in operating a business and includes both direct and indirect costs as described earlier. Expenses can include, but not be limited to, typing, telephone, automotive, travel, postage and delivery, lights, electricity, duplicating, and securing projects, i.e. writing of proposals, insurance. When you are employed by a company, it is easy to forget that paper and pencils cost money that you must now spend yourself.
Profit	Profit is your reward for business risks and ownership, and ranges from 10–50% of your salary, plus benefits plus overheads. Most business owners confuse revenue with profit.

Competition	When establishing your billing rate you must be aware of the customs of your community and of the industry. Many trade associations will publish current rates, and it is always worth talking to others in the industry to evaluate current market levels.
Economic conditions	Your billing rate must take into account the economic conditions that affect you. Is there inflation and/or a recession? At what rate are your costs rising or falling? When the market is doing well, this often produces a growth in the amount of consultants required. However, conversely, a poor economic market may not indicate the opposite. Often, when the market is going down and companies are reducing their work force, it may create more work for consultants to meet short-term needs.
Bad debts	A bad debt occurs when you are not paid for services you provide. Professional firms experience bad debt rates from 5–40%. Most try to maintain a 5–10% bad debt ratio. For ideas on how to ensure you collect the money owed to you, look at the section in this chapter: Limit Your Exposure to Bad Debts.
Fairness to clients	After considering all the above items, you must make an ethical judgment on what you think is fair to your clients and to yourself.

Calculating your billing rate

In this section we will be showing you how to calculate your base hourly billing rate. Many times you will not be charging clients on an hourly basis; you may use a fixed fee, but this step is important to provide the starting point in calculating other approaches.

Before the billing rate can be calculated, there are two important items that need to be defined:

◆ **Billable hours**. These are the number of working hours you *actually bill* to clients. You may work more hours for the client but you may not charge for all of them. The number of working hours in a year is estimated, simplistically, by taking the number of working weeks in a year, 48, and multiplying these by the approximate number of working hours in a week (41.66). The total of billable hours in a year therefore is 2,000.

◆ **Your utilization rate**. This tells you what percent of your total working hours each week/year that you bill to clients.

 – The target is to try to bill 50–60% of your available hours to a variety of clients.

 – The rest of your time (40–50%) is spent on looking for work, administration for your business, training, holiday, etc.

Foul!

If you bill consistently more than 60% of your time, other parts of your business will suffer, often the marketing side, resulting in the 'feast or famine' syndrome.

Therefore, if you estimate:

◆ a total number of possible billable hours at 2,000 hours

◆ a 60% utilization rate

you will only be able to bill 1,200 hours.

Setting your base rate

Setting your base hourly consulting rate utilizes your salary requirements as a first step.

Time out! The Rule of Two

◆ Your salary requirement is £...

◆ Estimated overheads, benefits, costs and profits = the same as your salary requirement.

◆ Therefore salary X 2 is your target revenue amount.

◆ To calculate your target hourly billing take your total yearly revenue and divide it by your yearly billable hours.

The rule of two is a simple and quick method to calculate your base billing rate. You only need to know your annual salary requirements and the number of hours you can bill to clients each year.

Example

If you require £40,000 a year salary:

◆ Multiply by two in order to cover profit, overhead and benefits = £80,000.

- You wish to work at 60% utilization rate (1,200 hours per year).
- The base billing rate would be £80,000 divided by 1,200.
- This equals a base rate of £66.66 per hour or approximately £550 per day.

In most industries there is an 'accepted' hourly rate, so the extent to which you can obtain the rate you wish depends on these industry standards. For instance, technical writing has a market place rate of £40, software programming can range from £60 to £80 per hour, and training consultants range from £1,000 to £1,500 per day.

Foul!

If you cannot achieve a minimum hourly rate of £40 per hour, you will be forced into working too many hours resulting in critical aspects of managing your business being missed.

Exercise 7.5   Calculating your target hourly rate

Work through the process below to help you calculate a base hourly rate:

Step one: what was/is your salary level in a full time position?

Step two: multiply this number by two and write it on the line below.

Step three: how many hours a month do you want to work out of a possible 160? How many days per month? What percentage is that of the total? Therefore, what utilization rate do you want to achieve? 50%? 60%? Write this number on the line below.

Step four: using that as a percentage of the total possible 2,000 hours in a year, calculate the number of billable hours you would like to achieve on an annual basis and write the number below (for instance 50% of 2,000 is 1,000 billable hours).

Step five: divide the figure in step two (the total revenue figure) with the percentage in step four. Write that figure below.

Step six: based on your knowledge of your type of consulting, how does this figure sound? Too high? Too low? How will you test out the validity of this target fee rate?

_____

_____

Time out!
Three factors determine your competitive position:

◆   What are your successful competitors charging?
◆   What will your clients pay?
◆   What minimum and maximum levels will you accept?

If your rate is perceived as too low prospective customers will assume you are not adding as much value. If your rate is perceived to be too high you may put off prospective customers: 'No wonder he can afford to drive a Mercedes!'.

Coaching point

Sometimes the figure can look too high when you first calculate it – remember, there are different ways of structuring fees so that you do not have to quote this as a daily rate, but which ensures you cover your minimum financial requirements (see the next section for more specifics).

Case study : Frank

Frank has sold some of his shares in one of his previous organizations to provide his back-up capital. He has built a clear cash flow statement based on the assumption that he will receive his first client within three months, and that they will pay their first invoice three months later. He wants to charge 50% deposit up front and then collect payment on the rest of the work later but he realizes that, as this is his first contract, he will probably have to hold off on invoicing up front this time. Frank realizes that most of his assignments will be long-term with a fixed number of days, so he has calculated that a daily rate of £650 for contracts over ten days in length is fair to the client.

Using different fee arrangements

There are certain common fee arrangements. Many consultants use different fee arrangements depending on the nature of the project.

Hourly or time charges

Hourly or time charges involve multiplying your billing rate by the number of hours you work for the client. This is the most basic and the most common fee arrangement.

All you need is your standard billing rate and a method to keep track of how you spend your time. The benefit to you is that you are paid for all the hours you work and there is minimum risk to you. The disadvantage to the client with this structure is that they do not know how much the project will cost, and have less control of the cost outcome. It can feel like a bottomless pit to them.

Case study

A client used a consultant on an hourly rate to develop three procedure manuals. All the money allocated to it was gone by the time the first manual was completed!

Fixed or project fees

Fixed fees occur when a particular service is performed for a fixed amount. The advantage to you of this fee structure is that it can hide your daily rate. The disadvantage is that you as the consultant run the risk of budget overruns, but you gain the bonus of budget underruns. Generally, if you quote a certain fee and it requires more time than expected you absorb the difference. Therefore you might be taking a risk and might not get paid for all the hours you work. Watch for the following:

- the project can change
- the client can try to add additional steps
- the client can change their minds
- the client cannot provide the information that you require.

To lessen your risk, you must have a very clear outline with the specifics of the project. In that way if the client asks you to do something extra, you can say that you would be happy to help, but since the terms of the contract have changed, you will need to negotiate for more money.

Coaching point

The rule of thumb for deciding how much to charge for a fixed fee contract is to take the numbers of hours you think the work will take, and multiply by two (minimum) or three (maximum).

Case study

A consultant was working on a fixed fee bid to upgrade existing applications and install several new applications, but because he had an incomplete understanding of the system requirements the installation went over four times the hours he had budgeted for the project. That type of project can kill the hourly rate!

Often customers enjoy this fee structure because they know ahead exactly how much the project will cost, which is normally of benefit to them in the budgeting process. This structure is also better for the tax authorities because they can see the project milestones, with a beginning, middle and an end.

Bracket fees

Bracket fees combine fixed fees and time charges. Essentially the consultant works on an hourly basis but his or her fee cannot exceed a specific amount. This fee structure favours the client and protects them from budget overruns.

Retainer fees

Retainer fees have several meanings among consultants.

◆ Retainer fees may describe an advanced payment to retain your services for a particular project. In this respect it is a sign of faith on the client's part to use your services and to ensure payment.

◆ In a slightly different sense, retainers are used to guarantee your availability during a certain time period. Clients pay you a fixed fee for a certain number of months to cover specific services. Clients use retainer fees to ensure continuity of services.

Consultants like retainer fees because they provide a steady income. There are also some challenges associated with a retainer. Clients may confuse a retainer with a salary, and overload your time. Conversely the client may become absorbed in their internal responsibilities and not give you the work that you have budgeted. While this looks positive in the short term for the consultant (being paid for not working!) in the long term this will cause the client to be dissatisfied and go elsewhere.

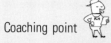

Coaching point

To try to ensure the success of this fee structure, make sure you specify in detail what is included and what isn't such as phone calls (how many), time at their site (how much), written communication required, etc.

This type of payment is common for such consultants as psychologists, legal counsel, etc.

Other less common fee arrangements

Fee type	Description
Percentage fees	Merger and acquisition consultants may charge a percentage of the entire transaction known as a percentage fee.
Assignment fees	As a consultant, you may perform projects that have intrinsic value beyond the number of days or hours consumed. Assignment fees are additional payments for such projects and can be either fixed amounts or percentages.
Equity fees	Occasionally consultants receive payment in the form of business ownership in the client's company. This may be an option if the client does not want to pay your published rate, however it is a high-risk option and you want to make sure you balance these types of high-risk compensation with firm cash payment.
Deferred fees	A deferred fee is not really a method of determining your fee. Instead it is a collection method that spreads the consulting fee through instalments over an extended time period. Deferred fees are used most often when the client does not have the money to pay you. The client may also request deferred fees so that the savings from the project can offset your consulting fee as it comes due.

Coaching point

If you are accepting deferred fees, you are extending credit to your clients. To offset these risks, you should consider the following tactics employed by many professionals:

◆ charge interest on the total amount

◆ charge higher fees

◆ request a sizable retainer fee before you start the project

◆ request collateral if your total fees are substantial

◆ request payment via banker's check or credit card to ensure payment

◆ be sure the company is solvent before you reach any agreement about deferred fees.

Exercise 7.6 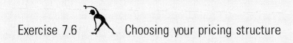 Choosing your pricing structure

Now that you have calculated your target hourly rate, let's think about what type of pricing structure would be best for you and the type of services that you offer.

◆ Based on the type of services that you offer, which type of pricing structure would you like to use?

_____

◆ What are the advantages to you of this pricing structure? What could be the disadvantages to the client of the pricing structure? How can you position this to the client in the most positive way?

_____

◆ How will you ensure you manage any disadvantages associated with this structure?

_____

Case study: Marie's pricing structure

Marie has calculated her base billing rate at £1,000 per day for large training and development projects. She will use this rate for quoting the sales training project she has proposed, as this will be a large customized programme. She believes this will cover some development and marketing time.

From this base assumption, for her other standard training programmes, she is going to charge per person per day, as this is a common practice in the industry. So she will charge a graduated scale based on numbers of people ranging from £100 per person per day to £150 per person per day.

She has contacted a training broker for whom she wishes to perform sub-contracting work. Although the training broker has over 40 large high-tech clients, she believes the exposure to these clients as she is getting started will prove to be extremely beneficial. She accepts that she will be paid only £400 pounds per day for this work, but feels that the corresponding benefits of gaining contacts and building client testimonials outweigh the revenue shortfall.

Quoting for extras

There should be no surprises on the invoice!

Make sure if you are going to charge for extras such as travel time, learning time, meals, etc that they are discussed and agreed upon up front. Many organizations will not pay for travel or mileage if you are travelling within the area that employees at the company come from. In addition, if you have to travel out of the country, consider charging a lower daily rate for that travel day. While you are not able to work the entire day, you may be able to complete some preparation work on the journey, so the entire day is not lost.

Guidelines in communicating fees to the client

Now you have established your fee rates and structure, how do you communicate these to the client and ensure that they agree to them?

Time out!

Asking for your rate

◆ The key influence on the rate that consultants can receive for their services is often their confidence in asking. If the client suspects from your body language that you are uncomfortable with the rate, they will try to negotiate to reduce it. If they hear confidence in your approach they are less likely to try to reduce the rate.

◆ Remember you can always reduce the rate: it is much harder to ask for more!

◆ Sometimes consultants are willing to ask for less money if the contract is in an area of interest where they receive the benefit of learning more. Make sure this is a conscious choice and the potential disadvantages are weighed against the potential benefits.

◆ Often consultants on long-term assignments give a price break on their daily rate. Remember if you do this that you will still have to build up your business again after you have finished the assignment, and you will need the money from that daily rate to do so.

◆ When you work half a day, you need to assess whether you can actually use the other half-day. Often consultants charge 75%-100% for a half-day for this reason.

Another factor to consider is consistency in pricing. Within certain market segments, e.g. high-tech, it is important to have a consistent fee structure. For different market segments, you may have a different pricing structure, e.g. charge less to non-profit organizations than to high-tech companies. Also, you may have reasons to take on a project that you know will cost you more than the amount the company has budgeted. If this is the case, you still need to do your best work, and not put in fewer hours because you are getting less than your regular rate.

Coaching point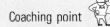

Many consultants fail because they under-price their services in the interests of building a client base and establishing credibility. If you have done your market research into current market rates, stick to your guns and ask. What you don't ask for, you don't get!

Collecting fees

Many new consultants assume that an invoice is the same as payment – it's not! It is possible to avoid many fee collection problems through good front-end communication.

Time out!

Collecting fees

◆ As early as possible, obtain a mutual understanding with your client concerning the fee. As a general practice, discuss your fees during the first meeting.

◆ Also, indicate how and when billing occurs. Many consultants find it difficult to discuss fees with perspective clients. Some fear losing the consulting project if their fees seem too high. Other consultants are reluctant to discuss money, and other consultants are so involved with discussing the project they forget to discuss the fees.

Limit your exposure to bad debts

Though you need to make an allowance for bad debts, there are certain things you can do to avoid not getting paid.

- Obtain progress payments by billing frequently. A business can budget a £1,000 per month more easily than it can absorb a £12,000 bill at year's end.
- Bill on time: the value of your service diminishes in the client's mind over time.
- Establish a billing and collecting practice.
- Make sure you obtain purchase orders (PO) wherever possible.
- Don't work without a PO.
- Make sure you have a clear contract with clear payment terms.
- Once the contract is signed, ask up front about the company's procedures for paying vendors. 'What do I need to do to get paid? What is your process?' 'Who has to sign off on bills?'
- Work in milestones throughout the duration of the contract.
- Ask if you can bill weekly/bi-weekly/monthly/bi-monthly.
- Communicate clearly your normal payment terms.
- Some consultants charge late fees. However, large organizations such as Sun and Oracle will not pay these.
- You may ask for a deposit up front.
- Check out the financial status of the company beforehand. Read trade publications, ask other vendors.
- Decide when to stop working if you are not getting paid. Many consultants have horror stories of being owed tens of thousands of pounds. Either set yourself a time period or quantity beyond which you will withhold services such as £10,000, or over 90 days. It is surprising how quickly a cheque can be written when you say you will stop working!

Your greatest friends in a company are those in accounts payable. Do not alienate them, but engage their help to solve your problem, if you are not getting paid on time.

Case study: Julia

Julia's first contract is with a small biotech start-up for 30 days' work, in two stages, with concrete measurable steps and deliverables for each step. Each step will be invoiced separately: the first step will be invoiced after five days' work, the second after ten days' work and the third at the end of the work. She has talked with accounts payable and built an understanding of their payment process. She knows she has to have a signed purchase order from the President, issue an invoice to the Director and at the same time issue an invoice to accounts payable (AP). AP then asks the Director to approve the signature and the invoice will be paid at 45 days. She believes that her knowledge of this system will prevent any exposure to bad debts.

Charging for sub-contracting

> The man who says he is willing to meet you halfway is usually a poor judge of distance.
>
> *Laurence J. Peter*

As we discussed in Chapter 5, one of the distribution channels for consultants is sub-contracting.

Time out!

Sub-contracting defined. Sub-contracting works both ways.

◆ You can sub-contract work to other consultants when you need help: this means that you are the main contractor and the other consultants are your sub-contractors.

◆ In addition, you can do work for another consultant, who has the main client contact. This means that you are the sub-contractor.

While this process is very beneficial both ways, it can also lead to misunderstandings if the working parameters are not set out clearly up front.

Sub-contracting work to others

When you have too much work, a viable option is to sub-contract the work to other consultants. Bear in mind the following guidelines:

- Make sure that you have worked with the consultants previously so that you know their competencies and their liabilities.
- Keep in mind that when you hire sub-contractors you are responsible for them and the work they produce.
- Be clear about the work they will be doing, the standards that you expect and the measurements that will be put in place.
- Be clear about the financial remuneration: see later notes, not only in terms of the amount to be paid, but the payment terms to which you will adhere.
- Make sure the sub-contractor realizes that all invoicing will be done through you.
- Make sure the sub-contractor realizes that this is your client. Any further work from the client, even if they sell it themselves, must come through you.

Foul!

Who owns the client?
Whoever sold the work, and got the foot in the door, owns the client. This is often the biggest bone of contention when working with sub-contractors. Most consultants do not realize the complexity of getting the initial entry contract and then want to own the remainder of the work. Some consultants use contracts to try to enforce this structure, but it is better to have a clear mutual understanding when you begin the assignment.

Case study: Peter

Peter sub-contracted a technical writing project through a business brokerage. He had to sign a contract stating that he could not work for that client directly for the next year. For this organization, there was only one purchaser of technical writing. It was appropriate in this case that he was unable to do business directly with the organization.

Case study: Marie

Marie began work for a large organization conducting training programmes. An organization for which she sub-contracted also did work in that organization, but with several different contacts. The brokerage tried to prevent the consultant from working with that organization, but that was inappropriate because the consultant had several direct contacts there, and there were multiple points of entry into the company.

Coaching point

The main differentiator on whether a client is yours or the other consultant's normally comes from the point of entry into the organization: did you have the first contact or did they? And that point of contact should be initiated by you, not as a result of doing work for someone else at the time.

Doing sub-contract work for others

This can be a good way to get work when you have time available and also when you are getting started. Sub-contracting is like the cake without icing. It enables you to obtain exposure, clients on your reference list and some stable income. However it is not as financially lucrative as working with clients directly.

Time out!

Following are a few guidelines about working as a sub-contractor:

◆ Make sure that you have worked with the consultants previously so that you know their competencies and their liabilities.

◆ Be clear about the work you will be doing, the standards that the contractor expects and the measurements that will be put in place.

◆ Be clear about the financial remuneration (see below), not only in terms of the amount to be paid, but the payment terms that you will accept.

Financial compensation for sub-contracting

The general standard in the industry is that the consultant or consulting organization which gets the work keeps approximately 50% of the revenue. The ability to market the service and collect the revenue is worth half of the total. Remember most consultants can do the work, but many cannot find it.

Exercise 7.7 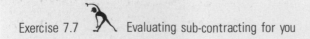 Evaluating sub-contracting for you

Think about how sub-contracting might fit into your service offerings.

- If you were overloaded, who could you use to support you? How would you structure the relationship? What written documentation might you need to confirm the working relationship?

_____

_____

- Who could you sub-contract for? What are the advantages to you of sub-contracting? What are the disadvantages of sub-contracting?

_____

_____

_____

- What percentage of your time would you like to spend sub-contracting for others? What percentage of your revenue should be spent sub-contracting? What is the minimum rate you will accept?

_____

_____

_____

Coaching point

Sub-contracting, when effectively managed, provides advantages as a relatively risk-free revenue source. Make sure you are clear about boundaries before any work starts.

Checklist

Have you:

- Estimated your start-up costs?
- Decided how you will fund yourself for six months to a year?
- Established financial objectives for your business?
- Created a cash flow statement?
- Calculated your base billing rate?
- Decided whether you wish to price your service by project?

- Decided how to limit your exposure to bad debts?
- Researched sub-contracting options as a base source of income?

Scorecard

Before moving on to the next chapter, think about the following questions:

- As you set your financial goals for your business, what is a realistic target revenue figure and how will you protect your cash flow as you are getting started? Think about what other financial safeguards you could put in place to fund your start-up.

- As you look at the industry, what do you believe is a the market rate for the type of services you are offering? Are your contract opportunities short term or long term, and how will this affect the pricing structure? What is the minimum compensation you will accept? What types of fee structures would be appropriate for your business?

- To what extent is acting as a sub-contractor to others a viable option for you? Who do you know in your industry who might have opportunities to provide you with work? If you do sub-contract to others what will be the lowest rate you will accept? Who do you know in your network whom you think you could use if you had too much work? What contractual arrangement will you have with these sub-contractors?

SECTION FOUR:
Getting Organized

Organizing Your Business

Game plan

Unlike when you work for an organization, there is no automatic structuring system when you are running your consulting business. The ability to organize activities and structure your environment is fundamental to being successful as a consultant.

The purpose of this chapter is to help you to:

◆ Set up your office space.

◆ Select the correct equipment.

◆ Identify any necessary outside administrative resources.

◆ Prioritize more effectively between multiple projects.

◆ Plan your weekly activity.

◆ Manage your paper flow.

Setting up your office space

There are two options open to consultants:

1. Work from home.
2. Set up a separate office.

Below are listed some advantages and disadvantages of both options.

Working at home

Advantages	Disadvantages
◆ Saves costs.	◆ Interruptions from family.
◆ Time effective – you don't waste time going from the office to home and back.	◆ No place to receive visitors.
	◆ Lack of professional image.
	◆ People think you're not really working.
◆ Avoids commuting: the two-second commute!	◆ Separate phone lines are essential.
◆ Most work can be performed from home.	◆ Difficulty in distancing yourself from the business.
◆ Fewer 'work' clothes.	◆ Self-discipline is essential to avoid temptations such as nice weather, soap operas and nibbling from the refrigerator!
◆ You can look like Edward Scissor Hands when talking to clients and they would not know!	
◆ Flexibility in that you can work your own hours.	◆ Work may 'spill out' through other areas of the house.
◆ It allows you to try out consulting without making any long-term commitments in terms of leases and rents.	◆ Office space can act as a 'red flag' to the tax man if you claim deductions for a home office.
	◆ There can be complications when you sell the house, because you are now selling a house and an office.

Case study: Marie works at home

Marie has decided to work at home, and has created a dedicated office space in what used to be the dining room. This is separated from the rest of the house, so she has the advantage of being able to close off the office when she is not working. It is a light area with easy access to phone lines. She learned from the first time as a consultant that her family tended to forget that she was working when she was at home, so she made sure this time that she established ground rules around office hours and break times.

Working from an office

Advantages	Disadvantages
◆ Separate from home.	◆ Cost.
◆ Prestige.	◆ Distance from home – commute.
◆ Proximity to clients.	◆ Less convenient when you want to refer to paperwork.
◆ Referral potential.	

Exercise 8.1 Will you work from home or rent an office?

Thinking about your consulting business, look at the advantages and disadvantages listed above.

◆ What would be the advantages to you of a home office? What could be the challenges? How would you overcome these challenges?

_____

_____

◆ What would be the advantages to you of an office out of the home? What could be the challenges? How would you overcome these challenges?

_____

_____

◆ As you are getting started, which option will you select?

_____

_____

Time out!
There are many ways to establish an office out of the home:
◆   Rent a small office.
◆   Share an office with other professionals; you may even be able to barter services for space.
◆   Use an executive suite.
◆   Sublet an office.

Coaching point
The key factor to remember when making the decision on office space is to ensure you have a dedicated space and you can separate/close off the office area from your home. Trying to share a children's bedroom is not conducive to productive work. Often when consultants are beginning their consulting practice, working at home is the simplest, most expedient option, and to this end it is worth working out ways to overcome the disadvantages.

Furniture

Consultants normally require minimal office furniture although the quality of the chair is key:

◆ desk
◆ chair
◆ filing cabinets
◆ bookshelf.

Just remember additional factors such as light and noise. The more aesthetically pleasing your office the more productive you will be.

Selecting equipment and support tools

Today's consultants require an increasing array of technology in order to be productive:

◆ telephone
◆ mobile phone
◆ answering services
◆ email
◆ fax machine
◆ computer
◆ printer/scanner
◆ software programs
◆ stationery.

Telephone

It is essential to have both a dedicated telephone line and a line dedicated to the fax and email when working from home. Often consultants use three dedicated lines: one for a business line, one as a fax line and one for email. Sharing a home line can cause inconvenience to other family members and might appear unprofessional. ISDN and cable lines are also an option.

Mobile phone

Mobile phones provide additional flexibility when travelling, however the roaming charges can mount up. So when you are looking at options, consider the extent to which you travel, and the degree of international travel before making decisions.

> Time out!
> There are decreasing costs and increasing competition in the telecommunications industry so make sure you shop around and read the small print in fee structures!

Answering services

Some type of answering service for your telephone is necessary to ensure you do not miss important business calls. The following are some of the options available to you.

- Answering machine with remote dial-in capabilities: while this is cheaper, the quality of the voice message is often not high.
- Answering service: high cost and hard to guarantee the quality.
- Voicemail: this provides the highest quality reception and most flexibility in terms of remote checking and saving of messages.

Email

> 75% of Britain's self-employed use email for work – compared to 16% of the public as a whole.
> *Alodis/MORI poll, 2000*

As the World Wide Web expands, some type of email system is critical. It can be used for researching companies, for marketing, for maintaining contact with individuals when you are busy and following up on proposals. The email provider does not need to be the same provider as the Web site provider. There is a broad range of paid and free email providers including BT, Yahoo!, Lycos and AOL. Talk to colleagues to research the providers that are currently available.

Fax machine

Having access to a fax machine is essential in today's business market. Options include either a stand-alone machine or a computer-based version.

Stand alone fax

Advantage	*Disadvantage*
◆ The stand alone fax works whether the computer is on-line or not.	◆ Material is received, but not in soft copy format.

Computer fax

Advantages	*Disadvantages*
◆ Documents are sent directly from computer to computer. ◆ You will have the soft copy of faxed documents.	◆ Slightly more inconvenient to use. ◆ If the computer is not on, documents cannot be sent or received.

As with other business decisions it is important to analyse the business requirements and then decide the best tool for the needs.

Personal computer

It is essential for a consultant to own a personal computer. The choice between an IBM (or IBM clone) or a Macintosh depends on the nature of the work you perform, your degree of computer literacy and the equipment your prospective clients use.

PC advantages	*Mac advantages*
◆ Wide choice.	◆ More user friendly.
◆ Clones can be cheap.	◆ Greater range of graphics programs.
◆ More complete range of software programs.	◆ Higher quality product.
◆ More companies use PCs.	

Time out!

Have you considered a laptop rather than a desktop computer?

◆ Prices of laptops have reduced drastically.

◆ Portability provides greater flexibility.

◆ Ideal if you want to work in multiple locations and/or client sites.

◆ You can buy a docking station so that, when you are in your office, you can have a screen and full sized keyboard.

◆ Laptops can weigh as little as 1.5kg so are lighter to carry than they used to be.

Foul!

Capacity does matter! When selecting a computer, more is normally better. More megahertz (speed), more random access memory (RAM – more flexibility in the moment) and more gigabytes (permanent storage).

Printer/scanner

A laser printer is an ideal investment depending on the number of written documents you need to produce. Many of the printers available now have colour printing options, built in scanners and can serve multiple purposes as a copying machine. Your choice of printer is related to the type of business that you operate.

Software programs

Below are some of the programs you will need and find useful.

Purpose	Type and Comments
Word processing	The most popular version on the market is Microsoft Word, which has largely taken over the market from Word Perfect.
Spreadsheet	Lotus 1-2-3 and Excel are the most widely used.
Database	ACT is an excellent sales tracking system. Access is also available in the Microsoft office suite, which is therefore compatible with Microsoft Outlook (for email). You can also use a more elementary Labels program. The purpose is to ensure you have a computer record of all prospects and clients. Read more about the requirements for a database in Chapter 5.
Presentations	Dependent on the nature of the graphics you need to produce; popular packages are Harvard Graphics, Page Maker and Power Point.
Cash management	Software, such as Quick Books, help to track finances, including revenue and costs.
Virus prevention	With the increasing volume of email comes an increasing number of viruses, programs specifically designed to harm your files. The two leading market providers for virus protection are Mac Afee and Norton Anti Virus, both of which can be downloaded from the Web.

Case study: Frank

Frank has purchased a laptop computer because this will provide him with additional flexibility when he is working on long-term projects. Most of this time is spent on the client's site. In addition, he has purchased a portable printer to supplement his laserjet printer in the office. He has then purchased a separate keyboard, screen and mouse for when he is working in his home office. He prefers an electronic fax machine, because many of the documents he faxes need to come directly from his machine, plus he likes to incorporate information from his client's tracking system into his report, and this means he does not have to double enter data. He has purchased an international cell phone, and set up two lines in his office, one for the landline and one for dial-up purposes. He has postponed signing up for Broadband until he is a little more settled. His laptop computer came complete with Microsoft Office and he finds this has been sufficient for most of his software needs.

Stationery and image

Stationery is the primary means of establishing a professional image and identity. It is often a good idea to keep it flexible to allow you to adapt the content as the business develops. The types of stationery and guidelines for using it include:

Business cards	◆ Use quality paper.
	◆ Err on the side of being conservative (based on profession).
	◆ Include name, company name, telephone number, fax number, email address and type of consulting.
Letterhead	◆ Same quality, paper and layout as business card.
Envelopes	◆ Keep the same quality, paper and layout as the letterhead. You can also provide labels that can be used on any type of envelope.
Clothes and image	◆ Your clothes and accessories need to match who you are, the image you wish to portray based on your area of consulting and your prospective client base.

Coaching point

Remember people buy people! Don't become too absorbed in design and layout. More importantly, many written communications are sent by fax and email, and therefore the quality of the written materials has become less important.

Example: image

A marketing consultant in the Midlands dressed in clothes such as a purple jacket and yellow trousers – no one doubted that he was in the design business!

Exercise 8.2 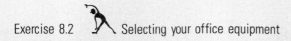 Selecting your office equipment

Take a moment to complete the table below to help you select what equipment you need in order to be productive.

Category	Questions	Actions
Telephone	Will you need a land line and a mobile phone? To what extent do you travel? How important is it to have international calling capabilities?	
Answering services	What answering services do other consultants use? Will you use an answerphone and message service or some type of voice messaging service?	
Email	What are your critical requirements for email? How can you ensure your email works when you are remote from your office? What email provider are you going to use?	
Fax machine	What are the benefits to you of a stand alone fax machine? What about a computer based fax system?	
Computer	Do you prefer a PC or a Macintosh? Do you need the flexibility that a laptop computer could provide? What capacity do you require? Speed? What type of computer do your prospective clients use?	
Printer/scanner	What type of documents do you expect to be printing? How important is colour in your printing requirements? How important is speed?	
Software programs	To what extent do you need to use word processing? Graphics? Spreadsheets?	
Stationery	To what extent do you think you will need stationery? How much of your communication do you expect do be conducted via email?	

Coaching point

Make sure you are economical when you get started. Better to be more cautious and add equipment later, than to burn through your cash reserves buying elaborate 'bells and whistles'.

Identifying administrative resources

One of the greatest challenges for the new consultant is the inordinate amount of time consumed by detailed administrative tasks.

Time out!

Remember Pareto's Principle:

◆ 20% of time produces 80% of results.

◆ 80% of time produces 20% of results.

Administrative tasks certainly fit in the latter category!

Often we cannot cope with all our administrative requirements ourselves or we choose to outsource them so that we increase our overall productivity and revenue. Options include:

Do it yourself	This is okay if you are computer literate and it also depends on the kind of work you do.
Temporary agency	Most areas offer administrative support services. Try to ensure the software used by the agency is compatible with your software so that business information is interchangeable. Some agencies will not supply resources if you work from home because of liability concerns.
Executive suite	Often the services of a typist are available at extra cost at an executive suite.
Contractual administrative support	Many consultants will invoice clients for the administrative support they need, at the cost they pay, or with a minimal mark-up. This ensures a win–win solution. The client pays a lower rate than if the consultant does the work. The consultant does not take on any additional expenses.

Company-provided Many organizations will supply internal editing and
administrative support administrative support in projects if this reduces the overall cost of
the assignment.

Employed staff This may prove to be too expensive and there may be not enough
work, at least at the beginning, to justify a salary. In the early
stages of your practice, you probably will have no need for
employed staff. The general rule applies that you only need
personnel if you are billing over 80% of your time, or if you can bill
over 70% of that person's time.

Case study: Julia

Julia did not think her time was best used fulfilling administrative functions and, as she built
her client base, she applied two different alternatives to the issue.

◆ One client had an internal junior HR person, so Julia negotiated that she would only
charge for the strategic advice and the detailed implementation would be performed
by the internal person.

◆ Julia's administrative assistant from a previous company had left at the same time
as she had and was not working full-time. For one client, she included her in the
project proposal.

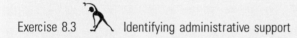

Exercise 8.3   Identifying administrative support

Thinking about your consulting business, answer the questions below:

◆ What type of administrative functions are associated with your consulting business?
For instance, ordering? Packing? Creating memos?

_____

_____

◆ Which of these is it essential that you complete? Which could be delegated to
others? What would be the benefits of delegating to others? What would be the
benefits of doing this work yourself?

_____

_____

◆ Which tasks therefore, if any, will you attempt to delegate? What alternative
resources could you use for each type of task or activity?

_____

Coaching point

If you are not sure how much time you spend on administrative tasks, or what these tasks are, you could complete a time log for a few days. Simply write down each task you complete and how long each task takes.

Prioritizing between multiple projects

We say we waste time, but that's impossible. We waste ourselves.

Alice Bloch

One of the greatest challenges consultants face is prioritizing between the multitude of tasks and projects to be completed. Because you tend to have to do everything, it can sometimes feel you end up doing nothing! A technique that can help in prioritizing is the **important/urgent** methodology.

Foul!

Most of us live our lives with the 'urgency habit' rushing from one activity to the next, with no time for pause or reflection. As we do this, we believe we are being efficient and getting a lot done. However, being efficient is not the same as being effective.

Time out!
◆ Being efficient means crossing tasks off the list by completing them correctly, quickly and with minimal effort. But many of the tasks we address should not be completed at all, as they were not even important in the first place.
◆ Being effective is what matters in improving consultant productivity. Effectiveness means that you are doing the right things, those things that will produce results, build your business and increase your revenue. In other words, focusing on the tasks and milestones that make a critical contribution to your consulting objectives and vision.

Whenever we have to prioritize between tasks and objectives, we need to ask ourselves two critical questions:

1. Is it urgent?
2. Is it important?

From these two questions we can create four quadrants:

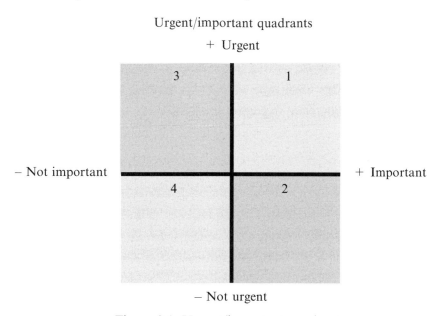

Figure 8.1. Urgent/important quadrants.

Quadrant one: important and urgent – quadrant of necessity

Many of your tasks fall into the **urgent/important** quadrant. These tasks represent your top priorities. Examples of tasks in this category can include critical reports, meetings to gather data, key deliverables, creating proposals and responding to client requests. Few would argue that tasks in this quadrant should be, and normally are, rated as number one.

Quadrant two: important and not urgent – proactive quadrant

Tasks that fit into the **important/not urgent** quadrant include such things as long-range planning, product development, assessing new distribution channels, and professional development activities. These tasks are part of the 20% of work that produces 80% of results. Neglecting these activities for more urgent, less important tasks drastically affects your productivity. These tasks should be rated as number two, to be completed after the important/urgent items.

> Time out!
> What differentiates successful, profitable consultants is their ability to complete tasks in the proactive quadrant.

Quadrant three: urgent but not important – reactive quadrant

Examples of tasks and milestones that might be in the **urgent/not important quadrant** are some telephone calls and emails, solving last-minute problems, fires, interruptions and small short-term tasks. Often these types of tasks are reactive in nature. These activities distract you from completing more important proactive tasks and milestones.

> Foul!
> The challenge comes when trying to differentiate between the urgent/not important quadrant and the important/not urgent quadrant. Normally there is a tendency to do the tasks in the urgent/not important quadrant (urgency habit) before those in the important/not urgent quadrant. In our hectic lives, there is not always time to think about the weight of a particular task. Instead most of us respond without thinking as we dash from one project to another. As a result, we tend to be always reacting and the more important long-term projects either do not get done or end up being rushed at the last minute.

Urgent/not important tasks can consume 80% of our time, but only produce about 20% of our results. Tasks in this quadrant should really be rated as number three and completed after tasks in the important/not urgent quadrant.

Quadrant four: not urgent but not important – quadrant of waste

Tasks in this quadrant should be completed last, if at all.

> Time out!
> One of the key time management principles is 'you can't do everything!' Choosing what to *not* do is as important as deciding what to do.

Exercise 8.4   Prioritizing your tasks

Thinking about your consulting activities, fill in your answers in the quadrants (see page 193).

- What two activities this month would you put in quadrant one – the urgent/important quadrant?

- What two activities this month would you put in quadrant two – the not urgent/important quadrant?

- What two activities this month would you put in quadrant three – the urgent/not important quadrant?

- What two activities this month would you put in quadrant four – the not urgent/not important quadrant?

- What changes could you make to your activities to obtain a greater return on your investment of time? What tasks could you decide not to do? What tend to be your 'urgency habit' tasks in quadrant three? How could you reduce your reactive tasks and increase your proactive workload?

Case study: Joe

Joe conducted his analysis using the exercise above and discovered the following:

- He was pretty effective at completing his priority one tasks – he was quick and seemed to enjoy multiplexing.

- His greatest challenge lay in quadrant three. He loved to be busy and would often jump in to whatever was in front of him without weighing the priorities. He particularly responded to the phone and sent over 50 text messages a day to many of his network of contacts. Plus, he loved jokes on email – he discovered that he was receiving about 20 emails a week containing just jokes! As a result, he has been too busy to work in quadrant two: contacting marketing companies to investigate opportunities for strategic partnerships.

- As a result of this understanding, he reduced his text messaging, removed himself from some email distribution lists and prioritized phone calls to only suspects and prospects. With the time he saved, he was able to surface one strategic partnership which brought him in his first client with a revenue of £10,000.

Coaching point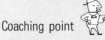

To improve individual productivity, make sure you prioritize your workload effectively to ensure time is spent in the important/not urgent quadrant, on those long-term important/not urgent tasks and milestones that drastically impact your business results.

Planning your activities

Until you value yourself, you won't value your time. Until you value your time, you will not do anything with it.

Scott Peck

Planning is the process by which we link what we want to achieve as a consultant (see Chapter 4 for business objectives) with when we are going to complete the critical tasks. Without linking our overall business direction to our daily and weekly activities, we will not optimize our productivity.

What to do?

Vision

Unique selling proposition

Key result areas

Objectives

What?   Tasks/milestone

Plan

When?   Month

Week

Day

Figure 8.2. Linking what to when.

Time out!

We plan for different periods of time:

◆ year

◆ quarter

◆ month

◆ week

◆ day

The further away the time, the less detail there is. For instance we need very little detail on an annual plan but considerable information on a daily plan.

Weekly planning

Steven Covey, in his book *First Things First,* highlighted the importance of weekly planning as an integral tool linking objectives and direction with weekly activities.

Activities planned and prioritised weekly could include:

◆ contact with customers

◆ essential milestones from key result areas

◆ meeting activities

◆ financial targets

◆ networking contacts

◆ marketing strategies

◆ new projects

◆ percentage of time in the office/on the road

◆ small 'don't forget' items

◆ paperwork/administration.

Coaching point

The weekly plan is like an organized, categorized, weekly to-do list.

◆ Plan the next week as you are moving though the current week. When action items for next week arise, put them on the weekly plan.

◆ Finalize your plan on Friday: this provides closure for the week and allows you to mentally prepare for the following week.

◆ Review your key result areas and pick out the critical tasks that need accomplishing that week. Full details on these project milestones will be in your objectives and key result areas. Don't write too much detail on your weekly plan.

◆ Write these milestones gathered under key result area in the two right-hand columns. These tasks are not, as yet, allocated per day (e.g. Xicor Proposal Team Building Programme is a task but it has no specific time allocated to it).

◆ Write in specific appointments (e.g. North Face meeting).

◆ Review the best times to complete critical tasks and book time for them on your weekly plan (e.g. Writing Team Building Programme is booked on Wednesday).

A sample weekly plan is given below in the case study. It is important to select your critical milestones to be accomplished before you set appointments and meetings, otherwise you are again working in quadrant three (not important/urgent) before quadrant two (important/not urgent).

Take a moment and review the sample from Marie's week.

Case study: Marie

Task of the week: Complete Intel Leader's Guide (L.G.)   Week of: _____

Date	Schedule	Key result areas	Weekly Tasks/Milestones
Monday	8:00 Intel Design Review 10:00 1:00 3:00	1. Clients • Intel • Oracle • North Face • NEC	Complete design LG Design Team Building Programme Meeting, finalize proposal Meeting
Tuesday	8.00 10.00 SGA Joe Smith 1.00 3.00	2. Prospects • Macys • SGA • Frito • Xicor	Call Meeting List of references Proposal Team Building Programme
Wednesday	8.00 10.00 1.00 Writing Team Building Programme 3.00	3. Database 4. Finance	Follow up call Add 10 new clients Invoice The North Face Monthly profit and loss
Thursday	8.00 NEC Bill Smart 10.00 North Face Mtg. 1.00 3.00	5. Marketing	Draft newsletter New contracts
Friday	8.00 Team Mtg. 10.00 1.00 3.00	6. Administration 7. Product development	Office filing system review Prepare first draft for 'Making Communication Work'

Exercise 8.5  Planning next week

Let's begin planning next week's activities.

◆ What critical tasks would you like to achieve next week? Think about networking, marketing, sales, business planning, telephone calls, proposals, projects, meetings, finance, operations, and administration. Write these tasks below.

_____

_____

_____

_____

◆ Now fill in your weekly plan on the following page. Fill in fixed appointments. Allocate time for specific activities where possible.

◆ How realistic is your weekly plan? Do you have elements from quadrants one to three on your weekly plan?

◆ What else do you need to do to plan your week?

Coaching point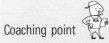

Remember, the thought process is key, the tool you use can be of your own choice. By planning your week in this manner you will increase your control of your discretionary time.

Daily planning

Time out!

Research has shown that if we have a clear picture of the next 24–48 hours, we will avoid stress and achieve more. Therefore having a clear plan of the next 24 hours can be important.

If you wish to plan your day, the best time to do so is the end of the previous workday. This gives you an opportunity to recognize the projects and activities completed and allows the brain to work on the next day while you are asleep!

Task of the week_____Week of _____

Date	Schedule	Key result areas	Weekly tasks/milestones
Monday	8.00 10.00 1.00 3.00		
Tuesday	8.00 10.00 1.00 3.00		
Wednesday	8.00 10.00 1.00 3.00		
Thursday	8.00 10.00 1.00 3.00		
Friday	8.00 10.00 1.00 3.00		

Many consultants, due to the nature of their work, do not plan every day. Some only plan 'office days' because when working on a client site there can be minimal time that is discretionary. Many of us use 'to-do' lists, but have a problem making them work because the list tends to be a random collection of activities. Buying groceries may be in the same list as achieving a major work objective! Make sure you use your weekly plan as the source of the critical tasks for your daily plan.

Coaching point

A suggested approach to daily planning is as follows:

◆ Each day *list all the activities* to be completed.

◆ Next, assess whether *any activities could be delegated, postponed or not done at all.*

◆ With the remaining activities, *assign priorities.*

◆ Estimate time needed for each activity.

◆ Estimate time needed for unplanned activities such as interruptions, fire fighting, and people demands.

◆ Judge whether you will need large uninterrupted blocks of time for the activities or if smaller blocks will be adequate.

◆ On a daily plan, assign a starting time to each item of work. Make sure you start on priority-one actions first.

◆ Match your work schedule to your body schedule.

◆ Don't over plan!

◆ Remember to build in regular breaks: the body can only concentrate for short periods of time.

On page 202 is a form that could be used for daily planning. Again, the thought process is more important than the tool.

Organizing your office work space

Organizing your office and paper flow is important in ensuring your productivity. There is nothing more frustrating than not being able to find a piece of paper! Often filing systems tend to develop in demand to paper, when they should help manage paperwork to achieve objectives.

Daily plan practice

Task of the day _____   Date _____

Schedule	To do
6:00	_____
7:00	_____
8:00	_____
9:00	_____
10:00	_____
11:00	_____
12:00	_____
1:00	_____
2:00	_____
3:00	_____
4:00	
5:00	**Calls**_____
6:00	_____
7:00	_____
8:00	_____

Time out!

A category-focused filing system consists of four main sections:

1. Current files relating to achieving short-term milestones.
2. Bring-forward files to track future actions related to objectives.
3. Current hanging files for paperwork related to current objectives: within key result areas.
4. Historical files for objectives: within key result areas.

Below are some guidelines for using each section.

1. **Current files: paper for today**. These can be sorted by objective, customer, etc and are usually stored on the desk, in stacking trays or folders.

2. **Bring-forward files**. Bring-forward files (sometimes called 'tickler files') can be located in hanging files or on the computer. Bring-forward files consist of numbered folders, one for each day of the month (31), and one for each month of the next six months (6).

   Requests for action are placed in the folder under the day the action must start. At the end of each day, you must check the folder to see what's coming up for the next day. Once each week, look at the folder for the coming month and move forward any items, which need to be in the 31-day files.

3. **Current project files: per key result area**. It is important to distinguish between current information, which needs to be readily available for possible action, and historical information which is complete.

   Current project files are normally located in your desk drawer and contain all current paperwork, divided by key result area, if at all possible. The files can be colour coded to indicate different activities, e.g. prospecting could be red, existing clients green.

4. **Historical data files: per key result area**. These files contain information which is complete and may be needed for future reference. There is a legal obligation to keep certain types of paperwork. The risk with historical files is that far too much information is kept, most of which is unlikely to be needed in the future. Historical files are also categorized by key result area and need to be cleared out at least once every three months.

Case study: Frank gets organized

Frank has begun organizing his office and has found that separating the historic from the current data has made it much easier to access paperwork. He has colour coded his filing system to correspond to his key result areas. He has converted the second bedroom at his house into an office, because he has the space and this is a cost-effective solution. When planning, he refers to his contact manager from the database to remind him of key people to call and follow up with, and then he creates a weekly to-do list for the additional critical tasks he needs to complete each week.

Exercise 8.6  Getting organized

Spend some time reviewing your paperwork and answer the following questions:

◆ How are you going to manage your current paperwork? On your desk? In a file drawer?

_____

_____

◆ To what extent will you use tickler files? Will this follow-up be stimulated by the computer? Or will you create a paperwork trail?

_____

_____

◆ How will you organize your current filing system? How will you cross-reference your filing system to your current planning tool?

_____

_____

◆ How will you separate current from historical files? How will you ensure that you continue to divide current and historical files?

_____

_____

◆ What else will you do to keep your paperwork organized?

_____

Coaching point
Organizing your paperwork will not only reduce your stress level, but increase your productivity. Remember you probably need to thoroughly clean out your files at least once every six months!

Establishing organization/administration objectives

You need to establish organizational objectives for your business within the administration/organization key result area. Again, these objectives need to meet SMART criteria.

Time out!
There is normally a variety of organizational objectives for a consulting business under several categories:
◆ office organization
◆ office equipment
◆ office location
◆ resources
◆ planning.

Exercise 8.7  Establishing organizational objectives

Thinking about your consulting business, create one organizational objective using the table below:

Key result area	Objective (s)
Organization	

Checklist

Have you:

- Chosen office space?
- Set up your office?
- Got the right equipment?
- Got the right software?
- Prioritized your monthly tasks?
- Completed a sample weekly plan?
- Identified a planning tool to help you in weekly planning?
- Organized your paperwork filing system by key result area?
- Established current files and 'tickler files'?
- Separated historic from current data?

Scorecard

Before leaving this chapter, ask yourself the following questions:

- As you set up your office, furniture and equipment, think about whether a home office or separate office would fit best with your lifestyle. If you are thinking of a home office, how will you ensure the effective division between your office and work? What other office options could you consider? What equipment will be the most useful to you in running your business?

- To what extent did you recognize the 'urgency habit' in the way you behaved? How can you ensure that you stop and think before jumping in to the task at hand?

- As you plan your weekly tasks and priorities, how will you ensure that you are concentrating time and energy on your key result areas? How will you link the overall direction of the business to your weekly tasks? What system can you use to facilitate this process? How else will you ensure that you are focusing energy into all aspects of running your business: sales, marketing, networking, product development, finance and administration?

- As you organize your office, what are the biggest challenges you face in ensuring your paperwork is easy to find and use? How will you overcome these challenges? Do you know anyone who can help you in this office organization phase?

CHAPTER NINE

Running Your Business: Doing the Work!

Gameplan

When you have successfully completed the key steps in setting up your consulting business described in Chapters 2 to 8, you will be ready to 'do the work': the area in which you have the most expertise. 'Doing the work' involves providing the functional expertise that you possess within the structure of a consulting assignment.

The purpose of this chapter is to help you to:

◆ Set up your contract with the client to ensure a win–win outcome.
◆ Understand the different types of contracts.
◆ Structure each stage of the consulting solution to ensure client satisfaction.

Formalizing contracts

Consultants, like everyone else, are turning to written contracts to protect their interests. Contracts do have a useful purpose other than self-protection. As has been stressed, the consultant–client relationship is ambiguous and a clear contract provides a guide for both parties. A legal contract is an agreement enforceable by law. Contracts can be written, spoken or implied. You may wish to send a letter outlining the responsibilities of each party in the contract. In addition, a verbal agreement is just as binding but more difficult to prove.

Time out!

When creating a contract you should consider including the following items:
◆ Responsibilities of each party.

- Time agreements.
- Financial arrangements.
- Products or services to be delivered.
- Cooperation of client.
- Independent contractor's status. This establishes that you are not an employee.
- Advisory capacity. This indicates that you will not make decisions for the client, but will provide best opinions only.
- Client responsibility for review, implementation and result.
- Your potential work with competitors.
- Authority of client to contract for your services.
- Attorney's fee clause.
- Limitations.

Coaching point

Using a legal contract is a personal decision. The majority of consultants do not use them. However if you have had problems with clients, or you are taking a substantial risk, then a contract is appropriate. Proper groundwork, continual communication and a thorough proposal may be an adequate substitute for a contract.

Exercise 9.1 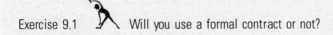 Will you use a formal contract or not?

Thinking about your consulting business, answer the questions below to identify whether you will use a contract with your client.

Questions to ask	Tips
Thinking about your client, to what extent have you worked with them in the past? How reliable have they been?	If they have tended to be trustworthy in the past and done what they said they would do, this is a good indicator that there may not be the need for a contract.
How large is the contract?	The larger the contract, the more need for a contract to protect liability on both sides.

How large is the company?	Often the larger the company, the more need there is for a contract. Most large companies have their formal contracts which they use when working with sub-contractors. As a consultant it can be easier to modify these contracts rather than insisting on using your own.
Thinking about the work, to what extent are they making business decisions that directly impact their bottom line based on your recommendations/input?	The greater the direct link between your recommendations and business costs/liabilities, the greater the need for a contract.

- As you consider the factors above, do you think you need a contract for your business?
- What do you need to include in a contract?
- Who can help you write the contract?

Case study: Julia

Because Julia provides advice about HR issues, with potential risks (eliminating certain positions and/or job roles, sexual harassment, etc) she has decided to always use a contract with her clients. With start-up companies, she worked with a solicitor to create a standard template to which she could simply add client details. This saves her the cost of having to consult with her solicitor for every contract. She has also found one lead in a large company where they have an existing contract. She asked her solicitor to review that contract to ensure that her interests were protected.

Structure of consulting assignments

There are broadly three types of consulting assignments:

- one-off projects
- short-term contracts
- long-term contracts.

The type of consulting you provide will often influence the type of contracts you receive. Marketing projects will probably be a mixture of short- and long-term projects, where training could be a series of one-off projects.

One-off contracts

These contracts take the least planning: a simple proposal normally acts as the project plan. They normally take place in a very short time frame: one to two days. Examples could be running one training programme for a team, reviewing a service level agreement and making recommendations, editing one document, etc.

Advantages	Disadvantages
◆ Give you variety of activities with different clients – greater client exposure.	◆ Can take as much time to sell as a long-term contract.
◆ Provide you with the opportunity to try out working with the client.	◆ Working with many such contracts can feel like a new job every day.
◆ May act as a marketing possibility to obtain other work with the client.	◆ Can be hard to keep all the balls up in the air.
◆ More clients for your client list.	◆ Necessitates keeping contact with more people.
◆ Simple to deliver and meet expectations.	◆ May not allow you to work in depth with the client and demonstrate the range of your competence.

Short-term contracts

Short-term contracts normally have a defined beginning, middle and an end, normally ranging from three to ten days. These short-term contracts require slightly more planning (some of this planning can normally be charged to the client) yet still remain fairly flexible in nature.

Advantages	Disadvantages
◆ Give you variety of activities with different clients – greater client exposure.	◆ If there are too many projects at one time, they can be difficult to manage.
◆ Easier to balance workload: two or three projects at one time.	◆ There is still an element of balancing multiple activities.

- One client does not dominate your time: keep other options open.
- Build reasonable client relationships over a period of time.

- If all clients want more work at one time you may be unable to meet the demand.
- Harder to sub-contract to others.

Long-term contracts

Long-term contracts normally have a defined beginning, middle and an end, normally ranging over 10 days with a series of specific milestones and deliverables. These long-term contracts require more extensive planning (some of this planning can normally be charged to the client) and often need to be regularly monitored.

Advantages

- Give you focused effort with one client – can feel more like a 'normal job'.
- Able to build a strong relationship with many contacts within one client.
- Can learn more about the company and therefore ensure that the consulting is linked to business objectives.
- Ideally situated to continue to develop more business.
- When you have established the payment cycle, you will normally receive regular financial payments.

Disadvantages

- If the project absorbs more than three to four days per week, marketing to other clients can suffer. A 'famine' may occur at the end of the 'feast'.
- There may be tax implications associated with being an employee.
- If the company experiences financial difficulties, then your entire source of revenue can be affected.
- You may miss other opportunities because of the lack of flexibility in your schedule.

Case study: Marie

Marie has decided the best mix for her business is a mix of one-off standard training programmes, and short-term projects. For one-off training programmes she will work through the training broker, as this will reduce her sales and marketing time, yet still provide her with a diversity of projects. She decides to focus on time management and presentation skills standard programmes in the beginning, because she has existing materials developed, plus she knows two people who could help meet client needs, if she is busy when they need help.

For the sales training project, she has quoted it as a short-term project with critical stages defined in the planning stage as:

- initial design

- pilot programme
- revision to class
- train trainers through the programme
- write leader's guides
- present the trainer programme for facilitators
- measure training effectiveness.

She believes that this will amount to approximately 15 days of training, but will be concentrated into a month. She thinks that there may be an opportunity to link the sales training programme with increases in sales. With this balance of business, she thinks that she will have some solid income, but will also be able to open up doors for further training when she conducts the standard training programmes.

Exercise 9.2 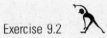 What type of consulting projects are the best fit with your business?

Thinking about your consulting business, identify what type of consulting projects, or mix of consulting projects, might be the best for you.

- To what extent would you have the opportunity to do one-off projects? What are the benefits that this would provide to you? What about the potential downside? How could you manage these challenges?

_____

_____

- To what extent would you have the opportunity to do short-term projects? What are the benefits that this would provide to you? What about the potential downside? How could you manage these challenges?

_____

_____

- To what extent would you have the opportunity to do long-term projects? What would you enjoy about such projects? What would be your main concern?

_____

_____

- What would be your ideal balance in percentages between one-off, short-term and long-term projects?

_____

_____

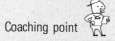

Coaching point

The more specific you are in what you want, the more likely it is that this will happen. Probably the best solution is to have a combination of all types of projects, to minimize risk and maximize the benefits of each.

Consulting project stages

Within each consulting assignment there may be a mixture of the following phases:

◆ planning
◆ needs assessment
◆ recommending options
◆ implementing recommendations
◆ monitoring progress
◆ evaluating success.

Depending on the type of consulting that you are providing, you may use some or all of the stages described in more detail below.

Planning the assignment

The time taken to plan the assignment will be directly linked to the time spent delivering the project.

Foul!

Planning is not a waste of time! Often time spent planning will increase the productivity and reduce execution time – a way to make your consulting business more profitable!

For one-off and short-term projects, the assignment is often planned in the proposal stage: basically you want to know who is going to do what, when, where and how.

Time out!

With long-term projects, you will need to be more specific, particularly in the early stages while credibility is being built on deliverables and milestones. Make sure you:

◆ Build in smaller, short-term deadlines: for instance in the design of a training project, copying the client in on the initial draft of training materials.

◆ Design an initial break-through project that has a high probability of success, such as a needs assessment in the development of a training programme.

◆ Break a project into smaller do-able tasks.

Needs assessment

In most consulting assignments you need to gather all the pertinent facts or data relating to the situation. You begin the data gathering and normally determine the primary problem in the initial interview. During data gathering you must also gather information about problems which the client has not shared with you.

Time out!

There are six basic data gathering tools:

Literature search: reading any published information on the company.

Document review: reviewing all internal documentation such as operating plans and procedures, along with external documents such as financial reports from auditors, banks, etc.

Interviews: gathering information from a variety of personnel within the company, by using a structured plan, and probing on specific issues. The dynamics are very similar to the sales interview process where you must relax the interviewee, build trust and obtain the necessary information.

Questionnaires: questionnaires can be distributed both internally and externally. They can be open-ended, requiring the respondent to write in answers, or objective, where the respondents have to rate given answers.

Direct observation: nothing can replace your own observation.

Basic research: some projects require controlled scientific research to collect the necessary data.

Recommending options

For specific types of client engagements, the information you have gathered from a variety of sources now needs to be analysed and synthesized to produce an accurate picture of the client situation.

Time out!

The steps are as follows:

1. Often, the data is analysed by reviewing any statistical data (the quantitative analysis), and by using a more subjective analysis from interviews and questionnaires.
2. When synthesizing the data you are attempting to produce a coherent picture providing the areas most in need of your and your client's attention.
3. Then the elements of the data are compared, prioritized and sequenced to be combined into a meaningful whole and often may be presented in a comprehensive report.

The options are normally presented to the client for prioritization and implementation planning.

Coaching point

Remember, when developing recommendations, options can be evaluated into one or more of the following four categories:

- client must do
- client wants to do
- client can do
- client should do.

Despite our personal opinions, normally the client has the ultimate decision-making authority!

Case study: Frank

Frank has received a go-ahead for the Support Centre reengineering project. He has outlined two main steps for the project. The first step involves conducting research into the current Support Centre operations, analysing current challenges and then recommending possible solutions. This step he estimated at four weeks – 20 days – at the conclusion of which he would prepare a report and present key findings to the management team. The second step involves the implementation of the critical recommendations. Phase One, he believes, will go smoothly because he will be meeting with key contributors and analysing Support Centre operations. This is pretty much in his direct control. He is somewhat concerned about Phase Two, because internal personnel are extremely busy and may not have time to invest in working on the implementation ideas. He wanted to try to ensure that changes were made as a result of his analysis. He considered providing support in this implementation phase but decided not to because he was worried about possible conflict of interest for future work. For instance, if this Support Centre assessment is undertaken on an annual basis, it would not be ethically fair for him to make the recommendations and then do the work – how could the client be sure the recommendations were not just to guarantee future work for him! As a great hands-on implementer, this was his first major experience of the difference between consulting (making recommendations) and working full time (making decisions and doing) for his type of work.

Implementing recommendations

Implementing recommendations is where the plan decided in the previous stage is delivered. Sometimes implementing the recommendations is the responsibility of the client and sometimes a consultant is used for implementation.

Time out!
If the client is implementing the plan, you can do several things to smooth the implementation process.
1.   Determine who is responsible for implementation.
2.   Understand the organizational structure.
3.   Train client personnel.
4.   Monitor the new system.

If you are implementing the plan, it is critical to manage the client's expectations and keep them abreast of any major changes to the deliverables. Often, in the implementation stages, clients are unable to dedicate enough time and resources to the project, and as a result deadlines might slip.

Case study: Joe
In Joe's consulting work, he found his role was not dissimilar to the role he played when employed by the company; he conducted the planning for his project, assessed options,

recommended design and marketing strategies and took responsibility for implementing the plan up to and including the product launch. Because of this focus, his accountant was concerned about the tax authorities thinking that he was really an employee, not a consultant. To overcome this concern, he actively looked for other one-off projects, for instance conducting market research into possible market viability for products, to ensure that he had a mixed client list. Plus he enjoyed the variety that this strategy presented.

Monitoring progress

Reports form an essential part of your communication with your clients. They may be the sole means of communicating with the client, and must contain all pertinent information relative to the progress of the project. Reports also facilitate clients' commitment to your work and give control of the project over to the consultant. There are two main types of reports:

- **The progress report:** Documents major events, problems and solutions.
- **The final report:** Documents the entire project, including background, methodology, findings, recommendations and conclusions. Often the final report is the only tangible result from the project.

Time out!

Major sections of the final report can include:

- table of contents
- executive summary
- project background
- objectives and scope
- methodology
- results
- findings and conclusion
- recommendations.

Evaluating project success

When you evaluate your performance both you and your client benefit. Evaluation acts as both a quality control mechanism and a learning device.

Time out!

Stages in evaluation are:

1. Deciding what to evaluate – for example:

◆ client satisfaction

◆ reduced turnover

◆ project outcome

◆ employee morale

◆ productivity.

2. How do you evaluate?

◆ collect pre-project data

◆ conduct evaluation immediately after project completion

◆ evaluate several months after project completion

◆ select appropriate measurement tools based on the project: interviews, questionnaires, observations, etc

◆ include the evaluation in the original proposal.

3. Documenting results

◆ present the entire picture

◆ document all results fully

◆ publish to other groups.

By evaluating success you can integrate learning into new consulting assignments while at the same time using them as a marketing tool to obtain more business.

Exercise 9.3  Outlining the stages in your consulting assignment

Thinking about the type of consulting that you plan to do, fill in the table opposite to provide the structure for your consulting projects.

Coaching point

Using this thought process with new and existing clients will help to ensure you do not miss a critical step thereby negatively affecting the outcome.

Step	Questions	Actions for you
Planning	How much planning is required for your consulting projects? How can you ensure you gain the maximum return from planning?	
Needs assessment	To what extent does your consulting work require that you conduct a needs assessment? Which combination of the tools outlined (literature search, document review, interviews, questionnaires, direct observation and other research) will be most suited to your client and your work?	
Recommending options	To what extent is your role to make recommendations, and not necessarily implement activities? How comfortable do you feel with recommending options without the power to implement?	
Implementing recommendations	To what extent will you be implementing the recommendations that you make? How can you ensure that you protect yourself legally and financially in this process?	
Monitoring progress	Will you be using a progress report and a final report? What would need to be the essential elements of your final report?	
Evaluating success	How will you evaluate the success of your consulting assignments? How can you make time for evaluation before jumping into the next assignment?	

Establishing project objectives

As with the other activities which you undertake as a consultant, it is helpful to define objectives for each project, as a way of quantifying the result you wish to achieve. Setting clear objectives for the project side of your business will help to ensure that you provide the services your clients require, and that will continue to develop your business.

Time out!

There could be a variety of project objectives under several categories:

◆ customer satisfaction

◆ productivity increase

◆ number of recommendations implemented

◆ critical milestones

◆ objectives related directly to the client needs.

The extent to which you can quantify objectives can vary from one type of consulting to another.

Case studies:

Frank's and **Joe's** consulting assignments are easy to set objectives for: an increase in client satisfaction and a successful product launch. For **Julia's** and **Marie's** business it is more difficult to quantify direct tangible results from a training programme or implementing an HR infrastructure because many other factors can come into play and affect the outcome.

Exercise 9.4 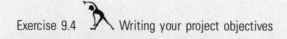 Writing your project objectives

◆ Take a moment and review the types of objectives you could write for a client project.

◆ Now write a SMART objective for one such client project below.

Key result area	Objective (s)
Client projects	

Checklist

Have you:

◆ Decided whether you will use a contract or not?
◆ Decided whether one-off, short-term or long-term projects are the best for you and your business?
◆ Gathered samples of projects you completed at jobs as samples for clients?
◆ Decided how you would like your work evaluated?
◆ Met with other consultants who do similar work to see how they manage projects?

Scorecard

Before leaving this chapter, ask yourself the following questions:

◆ As you consider your consulting business, to what extent will your business comprise one-off, short-term and long-term projects? How will you ensure that you capitalize on the advantages of each type of consulting work and how will you avoid any potential disadvantages?

◆ As you look at each specific project, how will you ensure that you put the correct process in place to ensure the effectiveness of each contract? How will you ensure your planning is effective? What will you do to keep the client informed on progress? How will you measure the success of the project?

◆ When you review your objectives for consulting projects, how clear are they as to the result that they will achieve? Who could look at them and provide you with feedback to ensure they meet the SMART criteria? Are there clear benefits to the client from the goals? How easy is it to quantify your objectives?

CHAPTER TEN

Moving Into Action

So what will you do now?

By this point you may be thinking 'What a lot of work!' Yes it is and No it isn't!

♦ 'Yes it is': consulting is not a 'magic pill'. Like many work opportunities it has inherent advantages and challenges. By understanding more about consulting and yourself, it is possible to make a successful alternative lifestyle as a consultant.

♦ 'No it isn't': many of these activities take place automatically when you are working. We don't necessarily think about them, we just do them. Think about your normal working day and how you do your job. If you tried to document that, it could look pretty scary!

For every person who says that they will never take a 'real job' ever again because they enjoy consulting so much, there are an equal number who, having tried consulting, return with enthusiasm to full-time work. There is no right or wrong decision: it is dependent on your needs and preferences.

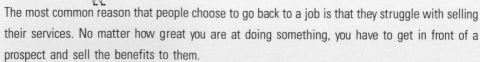

Coaching point
The most common reason that people choose to go back to a job is that they struggle with selling their services. No matter how great you are at doing something, you have to get in front of a prospect and sell the benefits to them.

In this book we have tried to share with you the critical steps necessary to establish your own consulting business, combined with exercises that you could complete to bring the ideas to life and make your business a reality.

In this book:

Section One covered **Getting Started**: to make sure you begin on the right foot.

◆ In Chapter One you were introduced to the dynamic business environment and understood why consulting is a viable and growing option for many individuals. It defined consulting, and gave parameters for the consulting industry as a whole. It included the following exercises:

   Exercise 1.1: What does consulting mean to you?
   Exercise 1.2: Would you benefit from working for a consulting firm?

◆ Chapter Two described the strengths and weaknesses of consulting as a profession, and showed the critical characteristics of successful consultants. Knowing the strengths that you bring to the role of a consultant and understanding potential challenges, can help you succeed as a consultant.
It included the following exercises:

   Exercise 2.1: Consulting advantages and disadvantages
   Exercise 2.2: Consulting advantages and disadvantages to you
   Exercise 2.3: Assessing your ability as a consultant
   Exercise 2.4: Animal characteristics
   Exercise 2.5: Choosing a mascot
   Exercise 2.6: Exploring temperaments
   Exercise 2.7: Is consulting for you?

◆ Chapter Three helped you to get started by defining your vision and unique selling proposition. In addition, by conducting SWOT analysis on your potential business, you were able to establish key result areas for your business that exploited opportunities and minimized threats.
It included the following exercises:

   Exercise 3.1: Defining your vision statement
   Exercise 3.2: Looking at your strengths and weaknesses
   Exercise 3.3: Defining your unique selling position
   Exercise 3.4: Conducting a SWOT analysis for your business
   Exercise 3.5: Deciding your key result areas

◆ Chapter Four provided you with more detailed skills and techniques to establish your business direction by writing a clear business plan, deciding the best business structure and being specific about expectations for your business by setting objectives and milestones. It included the following exercises:

Exercise 4.1: Writing your business plan

Exercise 4.2: Choosing your consulting business structure

Exercise 4.3: Writing your objectives

Exercise 4.4: Writing tasks and milestones

In **Section Two** we covered **Getting Clients**: the fundamental difference between being an employee and being a consultant.

◆ Chapter Five moved you from planning your strategy into business development mode, by introducing the key elements that you need to market your business and the promotional strategies that will raise awareness of your services. You were encouraged to formalize your network to ensure that you have the key building block for your business. It included the following exercises:

Exercise 5.1: Deciding your market research approach

Exercise 5.2: Deciding one marketing objective

Exercise 5.3: Deciding your market segment

Exercise 5.4: Defining your services, features and benefits

Exercise 5.5: Deciding your promotional activities

Exercise 5.6: Building your network

Exercise 5.7: Building your monthly marketing plan

◆ Chapter Six gave you skills and techniques in the most critical areas of success for a new consultant, selling your services. Using the telephone, face to face meetings and proposals you were introduced to the critical steps necessary to move the prospective client 'down the funnel' to become a paying customer. It included the following exercises:

Exercise 6.1: What are your fears about selling?

Exercise 6.2: Understanding your sales process

Exercise 6.3: Establishing sales objectives

Exercise 6.4: Which communication channel do you prefer?

Exercise 6.5: Preparing your 30-second commercial

Exercise 6.6: Preparing for a telephone call

Exercise 6.7: Evaluating your telephone effectiveness

Exercise 6.8: Evaluating your person-to-person effectiveness

Exercise 6.9: Deciding your proposal approach

In **Section Three** we examined **Getting Money**: you can have all the clients in the world but if they are not paying you, you might find it hard to live!

♦ Chapter Seven introduced you to the critical tools for measuring your financial business success and then gave you ideas on how to ensure that you charge enough for your services to make your business profitable and pay all the necessary overheads. It included the following exercises:

Exercise 7.1: What are your start-up costs and estimated monthly expenses?

Exercise 7.2: How will you fund your business?

Exercise 7.3: Establishing financial objectives

Exercise 7.4: Creating your cash flow statement

Exercise 7.5: Calculating your target hourly rate

Exercise 7.6: Choosing your pricing structure

Exercise 7.7: Evaluating sub-contracting for you

Finally in **Section Four** we reviewed **Getting Organized**: some basic principles for raising your productivity and increasing output.

♦ Chapter Eight provided ideas and techniques for organizing your business for maximum effectiveness. The following exercises would help you in this endeavour:

Exercise 8.1: Will you work from home or rent an office?

Exercise 8.2: Selecting your office equipment

Exercise 8.3: Identifying administrative support

Exercise 8.4: Prioritizing your tasks

Exercise 8.5: Planning next week

Exercise 8.6: Getting organized

Exercise 8.7: Establishing organizational objectives

♦ Chapter Nine talked about the different types of projects and how to ensure that they are successful. Finally we were able to talk about the part that most people associate with consulting – actually doing the work – with the following exercises:

Exercise 9.1: Will you use a formal contract or not?

Exercise 9.2: What type of projects are the best fit with your business?

Exercise 9.3: Outlining the stages in your consulting assignment

Exercise 9.4: Writing your project objectives

Exercise 10.1 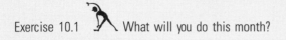 What will you do this month?

To help you decide your plan of attack for the next month, fill in the table below.

Questions to ask	Actions this month
Getting started: ◆ Have you analysed the strengths and weaknesses of consulting objectively? ◆ Have you decided your vision and established your key result areas? ◆ Have you defined specific measurable, time-based short-term objectives for yourself?	
Getting clients ◆ Have you begun to decide a marketing strategy? ◆ Have you conducted some telephone calls and face-to-face meetings? ◆ Have you begun to formalize and develop your network?	
Getting money ◆ Have you priced your product or service competitively, yet realistically? ◆ Have you decided how you will ensure the client pays?	
Getting organized ◆ Have you got yourself organized? ◆ Have you decided what type of projects are the best fit?	

Case studies

All our consultants have successfully launched their consulting practices, but in very different ways!

Joe has got going quickly by seizing the opportunity to work on a consulting basis for his previous employer. He is delighted that he is generating revenue right out of the door. His greatest challenge will be completing some of the strategic planning activities, which he views as unnecessary, but which provide critical guidance in long-term direction. He primarily used Section Two for ideas for getting clients.

Frank adopted a more methodical, structured approach, and completed Section One to ensure that he was clear about his offering before he presented himself to clients. His use of his network has brought him results surprisingly quickly — he didn't realize when he was at work how much people respected his output!

Julia has again adopted a more organized approach, with a focus on clearly identifying and articulating her business and marketing strategy so that her energy is focused entirely on relevant activities. She used all the sections of the book because she enjoyed the overview it provided to her of all the steps in the consulting process. As a business person, much of the content was a review of existing knowledge geared towards the consulting industry. She was pleasantly surprised at the responses and business she received from her mailshot to small companies.

Marie began forcefully with marketing. Having been a consultant before, she understood the pros and cons and was committed to making her consulting business work long-term this time. She used the funnel extensively to prioritize her contacts, so that she did not become overwhelmed with social rather than business focused interactions. The combination of using a distribution channel (training broker) and her own short-term projects has proved to be very successful.

If you follow the steps in this book, and are committed to trying the process, consulting can provide you with a greater control over your own destiny, more opportunities for creativity, the ability to make an impact and help you produce results for clients.

If you decide to return to full-time work, worst case you will have gained a perspective on a different lifestyle and gained some skills to help you back in work.

Good luck with whichever choice you make!

Scorecard

Before completing this book, ask yourself the following questions:

◆ Based on everything that you have read, be honest with yourself about how much you would like the constant multiplexing of projects, marketing activities and administrative tasks. What would work for you? What would be sources of stress?

◆ What are the benefits to you of consulting? To what extent will the benefits outweigh the potential costs?

◆ What are you going to do within the next month to either make it happen, make a decision or get a new job?

The Myers Briggs Type Indicator (MBTI)

The Myers Briggs Type Indicator (MBTI) was designed to try to assess which of Jung's cognitive processes we use most easily and then in what sequence we use them. It provides a four-letter code (e.g. ESTJ) which in essence, acts as a license plate to broadly describe how an individual might approach the world and the typical behaviors that they might demonstrate.

The Four Preferences

The Myers Briggs Type Indicator (MBTI®) attempts to assess our preferences on four dichotomies as shown below.

VISUAL The Four Preferences

DIRECTION ENERGY FLOWS

Extraverting	Introverting

FUNCTION: GATHERING INFORMATION (PERCEIVING)

Sensing	iNtuiting

FUNCTION: DECISION MAKING (JUDGING)

Thinking	Feeling

FUNCTION USED IN EXTERNAL WORLD

Judging	Perceiving

Extraverting and Introverting

Many analysts of personality think of Extraverting and Introverting in terms of where you *get* your energy: from the outer world (Extraverting) or the inner world (Introverting) but this is not how Jung originally described the two terms.

- **Extraverting** is defined as when your energy naturally first flows outward to the external world of people and events and then inwards to the world of ideas and thoughts.

- **Introverting** is defined as when your energy naturally first flows inward to ideas and thoughts, and then outwards to the world of people and events.

We have to live in both worlds! Just because an individual has an extraverting preference does not mean that they never reflect and allow their energy to move inwards. In the same way, just because an individual has an introverting preference does not mean that they never come out to interact! It is a matter of where your energy flows most naturally.

Now look at Extraverting and Introverting, represented by E\I in the diagram. Review the characteristic behaviors associated with an Extraverting or Introverting orientation in the chart below.

Extraverting and Introverting

Extraverting	Introverting
Often drawn out to interact	Often pulled in to reflect
Act first and then think (initiate)	Think first and then act (respond)
Process information in the external world – talk everything over	Process information in the internal world – think everything over
May be easier to 'read' Self-disclose readily	May be harder to 'read' Share personal information with few, close people
May talk more than listen	May listen more than talk
May communicate with enthusiasm	May keep enthusiasm to self
May use more expressive body language	Use more reserved body language
May respond quickly with a verbal stream of consciousness	May respond after taking time to think – more deliberate speaking pattern

Put an X by the orientation that seems most like you in the space provided.

My Orientation is toward: Extraverting (E) ☐   Introverting (I) ☐

Sensing and iNtuiting

Jung identified two main ways that we tend to gather or perceive information: Sensing and iNtuiting.

◆ Individuals who prefer the **Sensing** process, tend to primarily gather information through their senses such as sight, sound, smell, touch, taste, and balance. They also tend to trust whatever can be measured or documented and what is real and concrete. As a result, they may initially appear to doubt intuitive insights. They tend to use more concrete language, being more literal and using specific words.

◆ Individuals who prefer the **iNtuiting** process gather information through ideas, patterns, possibilities hypotheses, and inferred meanings. They also tend to trust abstract concepts, ideas and potential, minimizing the importance of concrete evidence. They tend to use more abstract language, being more general and figurative.

Now look at Sensing and iNtuiting, represented by S/N in the diagram. Review the characteristic behaviors associated with a Sensing and iNtuiting orientation in the chart below.

Sensing	iNtuiting
Tune into information that is concrete and real: see, hear, smell, touch, taste, and feel	Tune into information that is abstract or theoretical: concepts, theories, patterns and insights
Notice concrete detail like changes in someone's appearance; can be frustrated when others are oblivious to the concrete environment	Notice and interpret what's between the lines in communication; can be frustrated when others take things literally
Like to use tangible, physical, or practical skills	Like to philosophize and develop new concepts
Tend to be specific: give details and examples in a linear step-by-step approach or in literal form	Tend to be figurative with general descriptions and theories, using analogies and metaphors
Speak and hear literally	Speak and hear figuratively
Tend to present concrete evidence either sequentially or briefly and to the point	Tend to present information in impressions or organized around a conceptual framework without concrete examples
Move from specific to general: start with the steps and move to the end result	Move from general to specific: start with the end result and then build up the steps
Can appear realistic or too focused on the details	Can appear visionary or impractical

My information gathering process is: Sensing ☐   Intuiting ☐

Thinking and Feeling

Jung identified two main ways that we tend to make decisions or judge events: Thinking and Feeling. Both are rational decision-making processes, they are simply based on different criteria.

◆ Individuals who make decisions based on **Thinking**, tend to make decisions impersonally, logically and analytically. They may see criteria as black and white: 'the facts ma'am, just the facts!'

◆ Individuals who make decisions based on **Feeling**, tend to be more interested in subjective criteria such as personal values, the people involved, and special circumstances. They may see criteria as shades of gray.

Now look at Thinking and Feeling, represented by T/F in the diagram. Review the characteristic behaviors associated with a Thinking and Feeling orientation in the chart below.

THINKING	FEELING
Feelings need to be understood to be truly felt	Feelings are felt and often difficult to explain
Conflict can be intriguing	Conflict is gut wrenching
Need to be in control of their emotions	Like to be swept away in emotion, need to express their emotions
Logical analysis	Emotional intensity
Remember numbers and figures more easily	Remember faces and names more easily
Decisions are based on logical, objective criteria	Decisions are based on personal, subjective criteria
Definition of fairness is one standard for all	Definition of fairness is caring and based on personal factors
Others say I sometimes appear heartless, insensitive, and uncaring	Others say I sometimes appear overemotional, illogical and weak

My decision making process is: Thinking ☐   Feeling ☐

Judging and Perceiving

The final preference, the Judging and Perceiving Preference, was added to Jung's typology by Myers and Briggs to help to explain which function individuals use in the external world.

◆ Individuals with a **Judging preference** prefer to achieve closure, make decisions and make plans either to organize resources to achieve an end goal, or to push for closure to achieve group harmony. Therefore individuals with a Judging preference tend to like to make a plan and stick to it.

◆ Individuals with a **Perceiving preference** prefer to remain flexible, open to possibilities and enjoy exploring options from current concrete data, or generating possibilities and employing future patterns. Therefore individuals with a Perceiving preference either make decisions and change them easily (Artisans) or keep their options open and postpone making a decision (Idealists and Rationals).

Judging	Perceiving
Most comfortable after decisions are made and then stick to it	Most comfortable leaving options open or quick to change if circumstances change
Set goals and work towards achieving them on time	Change goals as information becomes available
Prefer knowing what events are coming up	Like adapting to new situations
Finish the task in a structured manner and enjoy the result	Enjoy the process and complete the task in order to move onto the next project
Deadlines are serious: time is finite	Deadlines are elastic: time is a renewable resource
Push for closure	Like 'going with the flow'
Tend to schedule time, plan and organize	Tend to be more spontaneous

Place an X in the box beside the orientation that seems most like you.

My Orientation is toward: Judging ☐   Perceiving ☐

Further Reading

Berens, Linda V., Ernst, Linda K., Robb, Judith E. and Smith, Melissa A., *Temperament and Type Dynamics. The Facilitator's Guide*. Huntington Beach. California: Temperament Research Institute, 1995.

Berens, Linda V., *Understanding Yourself and Others: An Introduction to Temperament – 2.0*. Huntington Beach. California: Telos, 2000.

Covey, S., *The Seven Habits of Highly Effective People*. New York: Fireside, Simon & Schuster, 1989.

Delunas, E., *Survival Games Personalities Play*. SunInk Publications, 1992.

Handy, C., T*he Age of Unreason*. Boston: Harvard Business School Press, 1990.

Handy, C., *The Age of Paradox*. Boston: Harvard Business School Press, 1994.

Handy, C., *Beyond Certainty*. Boston: Harvard Business School Press, 1996.

Hersey, P., and Blanchard, K. H., *Management of Organizational Behavior: Utilizing Human Resources*. Upper Saddle River, NJ: Prentice-Hall, 1988.

Hirsh, S., and Kummerow, J., *Life Types*. New York: Warner Books, 1989.

Isachsen, O., *Joining the Entrepreneurial Elite*. Palo Alto, CA: Davies-Black, 1997.

Kelley, Robert Earl, *Consulting*. Scribner, October, 1986.

Keirsey, D., *Portraits of Temperament*. Del Mar, CA: Prometheus Nemesis Books, 1987.

Keirsey, D., *Please Understand Me II*. Del Mar, CA: Prometheus Nemesis Books, 1998.

Keirsey, D, and Bates, M., *Please Understand Me*. Del Mar, CA: Prometheus Nemesis Books, 1978.

Kriegel, R. J., and Patler, L., *If It Ain't Broke, Break It*. New York: Warner Books, 1992.

Kriegel, R.J., Brandt, David., *Sacred Cows Make the Best Burgers*. New York: Warner Books, 1997.

Lakein, Alan, *How to Get Control of Your Time and Your Life*. New American Library, 1996.

Quenk, N., *Beside Ourselves: Our Hidden Personality in Everyday Life*. Palo Alto, CA: Davies-Black, 1993.

Quenk, N., *In the Grip: Our Hidden Personality*. Palo Alto, CA: Consulting Psychologists Press, 1996.

Tieger, P. D., and Barron-Tieger, B., *Do What You Are*. Boston: Little, Brown, 1995.

Timmons, Jeffrey A., *The Entrepreneurial Mind*. Brick House Publications. March, 1989.

Other reference sources

Barclay's Bank Research Review, *Starting up in Business*, July 1999.

Daily Telegraph, *Working for Yourself* Book.

Association of Management Consultants study 'Personal Qualifications of Management Consultants'.

I Want To Be My Own Boss – Inside the New Self Employed Revolution. Alodis/MORI poll, 2000.

Institute of Management Consultants, 32–33 Hatton Garden, London EC1N 8DL. Tel: (020) 7242 2140.

Federation of Small Businesses, Whittle Way, Blackpool Business Park, Blackpool, FY4 2FE. Tel: (01253) 336000.

Department of Trade and Industry, Department of Social Security, the Inland Revenue and Department for Education and Employment also print useful pamphlets.

Other books

Small Business Guide (4th edn), C Barrow Business Publications.

Be your Own Boss, David McMullan (Kogan Page).

Croner's Reference book for the self employed and Smaller Business, Croner Publications.

Going Freelance, Godfrey Golzen (Kogan Page).

Consulting workshops

Consulting and Making Money At It, contact EM-Power LLC, 9 Westwood Road, Marlow, Bucks SL7 2AT. Tel: (01628) 891481. Email: Susan.Nash@em-power.com

Business information

New Venture Creation (6th edn) Jeffry A. Timmons (McGraw Hill Higher Education).

Up Your Own Organization, Donald M. Dible (Roston Publishing).

Self improvement

First Things First, Steven Covey (Prentice Hall & IBD).

Index